CO-RULING WITH CHRIST

Practical Tools for Kingdom Dominion

© Copyright 2022, Hugh Daniel Smith. All Rights Reserved.

Contents

Preface

Part 1: Humanity's Dominion Mandate Fulfilled in Christ and His Kingdom

   1 - The Dominion Mandate
   2 - God Rules Through His Image
      The Power of Image
      God's Image in Humanity
   3 - The Distortion of God's Image
   4 - The Restoration of God's Image
      Christ and His Kingdom
      The Name of Jesus
   5 - The Four Levels of Power
      The Right
      The Might
      Inner Strength to Fight
      Governing Systems

Part 2: Conformity to Christ

   6 - Becoming Like Christ
      Identification
      Imprinting
      Imitation
      Impartation
   7 - The Five Laws of the Cross
      Substitutionary Death and Emancipation
      Substitutionary Burial and Purification
      Substitutionary Resurrection and New Life

    Substitutionary Ascension and Spiritual Gifts
    Substitutionary Reign and Power
    A Daily Practice
8 - Living and Ruling in Christ
    Partnering with Holy Spirit
    Measure of Rule
    Our Promised Land
    Ruling with Christ - Now to Eternity
9 - Miracles: Two Case Studies
    Case #1: Prophetic Alignment
    Case #2: Physical Healing
    Profoundly Simple and Simply Profound

Part 3: The Heavenly Council and Tools of the Trade

10 - The Heavenly Council
    Scriptural Support
    Decrees (Scrolls)
    "Cutting Realities" Based on Divine Decrees
    The Courts of Heaven
    The Ruling Church
11 - Tools of the Trade
    Decree
    Confession
    Meditation
    Declaration
    Proclamation
    Renouncement
    Promise
    Impartation
    Regulation
    Reconciliation

      Petition
      Allocation
      Dedication
      Vow
      Blessing
      Activation
      Confirmation
12 - Conducting Casework
      How to Conduct Casework
      How to Utilize the Tools of the Trade
      The Man by the Pool of Bethesda

Closing Remarks

Acknowledgments

Appendix: The Five Laws of the Cross (Original Legislation)

Preface

The question of human suffering has perplexed human beings for millennia. Some philosophers reason that suffering is not really a bad thing, for it offers people the opportunity to prove their true moral character. Some contemporary, secular thinkers conclude that God is either incapable of stopping human suffering, capable but uncaring, or simply nonexistent. Ancient Jewish writers interpret Israel's suffering as a form of chastisement for sins which required repentance and sacrifice. Hindus believe that human suffering is the result of karma, and therefore, people are encouraged to accept and endure it. The purpose of this book is not only to offer another perspective on human suffering but also to provide practical tools that can be employed in the work of healing and overcoming it.

In this book, we will explore humanity's Dominion Mandate and how it factors into the management and wellbeing of the earth. Leaders of companies and organizations, fathers and mothers, individuals and couples can all participate in healing our world by simply accepting this mandate and employing the tools of the trade. I truly believe God is raising up an army of believers who are adequately trained to co-rule with Christ - from His throne in heaven to the earth where we reside. The healing of our land will only become a reality when this army of co-rulers proves to this generation by demonstration that Jesus is not only alive but that He is Lord and Ruler of all.

Part One
The Dominion Mandate

Humanity's Dominion Mandate Fulfilled in Christ and His Kingdom

1 - The Dominion Mandate

From the beginning, we as human beings were designed and destined to rule with God. According to the Genesis account, when God created humanity, He blessed them, and He charged them to "be fruitful, and multiply, and replenish the earth, and subdue it: and have dominion over the fish of the sea, and over the fowl of the air, and over every living thing that moveth upon the earth" (Genesis 1:28, KJV). Some have called this assignment from God the "Dominion Mandate" - the divine command to sovereignly govern the earth in God's stead.

Despite the challenges that we face in our world today, God has always intended the earth to be a physical representation of heaven. On this terra firma, God will manifest His rule - His wisdom, His kindness, His beauty - so that His majesty will be displayed for all to see. Through human beings, God's plan is to "colonize" or "annex" the earth to make it look like heaven. This intent is echoed millenia later, when Jesus prayed to the Father, "your kingdom come, your will be done, on earth as it is in heaven" (Matthew 6:10, NIV). God wants to establish His Kingdom in the earth so that the entire planet becomes a paradise under His beneficent rule.

At one point in history, it was said that "the sun never sets on the British Empire." In other words, the extent of Britain's rule was so global that the sun was supposedly always shining on at least one of their territories or colonies. As the British Empire claimed and colonized other lands and people groups, it attempted to impose and establish its language, culture, and customs - to make each colony look like England. The colonizers would endeavor, forcibly if necessary, to cause the colonies to serve the empire and adopt its values. The British Empire often employed brutal tactics of subjugation to accomplish this purpose - including military domination, economic exploitation, and enslavement.

These are obviously not God's tactics for rulership and dominion of the earth, but God does intend to "colonize" the earth in His own way - to establish His rule and to make the earth look like heaven. So how does God establish His rule? How does He expand His Kingdom? How does He bring heaven to earth?

2 - God Rules Through His Image

Prior to humanity receiving the "Dominion Mandate," the Bible says that God "created human beings in his own image. In the image of God he created them; male and female he created them" (Genesis 1:27, NLT). We as human beings were made in the image and likeness of God. This means that we carried and represented His nature, character, and power. We facilitated His vision and manifested it in the physical realm. We were His emissaries, His ambassadors, His delegates. We were the link between heaven and earth. We shone the light of God's image, and we were imbued with His authority to govern. It was God's intent to rule over the earth through His image - through humanity - and to cause every good thing to flourish under His wise and loving care.

The Power of Image

The old adage says that "a picture is worth a thousand words." The scientific truth is even more dramatic: the human brain can actually process images up to 60,000 times faster than text. In fact, 90% of information transmitted to the brain is visual, and the brain absorbs and synthesizes visual information faster than any other stimuli.[1] It is therefore difficult to overstate the power of images on the human mind.

Advertisers are aware of this power, and companies spend a significant amount of time, research, and money to

---

[1] Eisenberg, Harris. "Humans Process Visual Data Better." *Thermopylae Sciences + Technology*, 15 Sept. 2014.

effectively brand themselves in the eyes of consumers. These companies attempt to create positive brand recognition. Brand recognition is "the ability of consumers to recognize an identifying characteristic of one company versus a competitor. A company is perceived as having successful brand recognition when consumers are able to recognize the firm through visual or auditory cues alone, even without hearing the company's name."[2] For example, when you are driving down the road and you see the "golden arches" in the distance, you know McDonald's is up ahead. Successful branding also elicits certain positive feelings, emotions, and ideas within consumers when they think about the company or the product.

In addition to branding for economic purposes, images have often been used as symbols of power and authority. Consider the images of the caesars that were erected and stamped throughout the Roman Empire. Or the statues and monuments that are built for military conquerors around the world. Or the images of the Founding Fathers on U.S. currency. These images are used to display power - the alleged right and might to rule. Though these historical examples are distortions of God's original intent, God's plan to "annex" the earth likewise required the presence of His image.

In many ways, we tend to become like the image that is raised before us - to become like what we meditate upon and what we worship. It was perhaps for this reason that the first two of the Ten Commandments in the Old

---

[2] Kenton, Will. "Brand Recognition." *Investopedia*, 10 Aug. 2021, www.investopedia.com/terms/b/brand-recognition.asp.

Testament warned about images or objects of worship other than God (see Exodus 20, NIV):

1. You shall have no other gods before me.
2. You shall not make for yourself an image in the form of anything in heaven above or on the earth beneath or in the waters below. You shall not bow down to them or worship them.

Images are incredibly powerful, for as we focus upon them, they have the power to shape or transform us into their likeness. The more we gaze upon them, the more we exalt them in our hearts and minds, the more we become like them. Consider this passage concerning idol worship and its consequence:

> But their idols are silver and gold, made by human hands. They have mouths, but cannot speak, eyes, but cannot see. They have ears, but cannot hear, noses, but cannot smell. They have hands, but cannot feel, feet, but cannot walk, nor can they utter a sound with their throats. Those who make them will be like them, and so will all who trust in them (Psalm 115:4-8, NIV).

As people made and trusted in powerless idols, they became powerless themselves. They became as spiritually blind as the graven idols they constructed.

Consider also the story of the bronze serpent from Numbers 21. The people of Israel had spoken against God and against Moses, and consequently, there were fiery serpents in the camp that were biting and killing many of the people. As the solution, God instructed Moses to fashion a bronze serpent and put it on a pole, and anyone who looked up and saw the bronze serpent was healed of the poisonous bites from the fiery serpents. When the people focused their attention on the "defeated serpent" nailed to the pole, they were healed and delivered from the power of the serpent in their physical bodies.

It was in the context of this story that Jesus said, "'Just as Moses lifted up the snake in the wilderness, so the Son of Man must be lifted up, that everyone who believes may have eternal life in him.' For God so loved the world that he gave his one and only Son, that whoever believes in him shall not perish but have eternal life" (John 3:14-16, NIV). The more we see Jesus, the more we are transformed into His image! For "we all, with unveiled face, beholding the glory of the Lord, are being transformed into the same image from one degree of glory to another. For this comes from the Lord who is the Spirit" (2 Corinthians 3:18, ESV).

God's Image in Humanity

All of creation was (and still is) wired to respond to the image or reflection of its Creator, and God created humanity in His own image and likeness so that we could govern on His behalf. We were meant to bear His nature, character, and power - to be facilitators and conduits of His perfect will. We were meant to bring and maintain heaven on earth.

Because God has given the earth over to humanity, He will not operate in the earth without some kind of partnership with humanity. God will always work with and through human beings when He wants to accomplish something in this physical realm. The covenants God made with individuals like Noah, Abraham, and David are indicators of this invitation to partnership. Once again, God made human beings in His image, so He chooses to work with human beings as His representatives and ambassadors.

We as believers must awaken to the power and authority that God has given us as His image bearers, and we must accept the invitation to co-rule with God. Too often, we defer this power to others, and we operate as if God will accomplish His purposes directly from the heavens without our involvement. This can sometimes show up in the way we pray, as well. But once again, God has chosen to accomplish His purposes through His representatives - through human beings. That means that in many cases, God wants to answer our prayers by empowering us to be the solution to the challenges we are facing. God has given us the power to rule - to declare what He has decreed, to operate in the supernatural, and to bring heaven to earth.

While some believers still need to awaken to the authority God has given them, others have recognized this authority but misunderstood and misapplied it. These believers are using the language of authority, but they are attempting to utilize this God-given power for self-directed ends and personal desires. They are not manifesting the image of God; they are manifesting their own image.

Therefore, a strong caveat must be made here. Humanity's Dominion Mandate (the power to co-rule with God) was given in response to human beings bearing the image of God. That means that the image of God is the anchor of co-ruling. For human beings, all legitimate co-rulership with God is contingent upon bearing the authentic image of God. When we are operating with the nature, character, and will of God, then we have power to bring God's will to pass. Without this, we are attempting to wield authority without the true source of that authority.

3 - The Distortion of God's Image

When humanity gave in to the serpent's temptation in the garden of Eden, when we ate the fruit that God instructed us not to eat, the image of God was distorted in humanity. We ate from the tree of the knowledge of good and evil, meaning that instead of allowing God to define good and evil for us, we chose to seize power and define good and evil for ourselves. In this way, the image of God was marred and defaced, and we forfeited our opportunity to effectively govern the planet.

Satan recognizes that God placed human beings in the earth to rule through the image of God. Therefore, the satanic agenda is to warp and distort the image of God in humanity and to replace it with his own image. The enemy wants to "hack" human beings and rewire them with his programming so that we replicate his values and his ideas. If humanity carries the image of satan rather than the image of God, then satanic power will shape the earth.

In many ways, our current global state of affairs is a reflection of the distorted image of God in humanity. Famine, war, disease, injustice, and oppression are the results of a satanic image being promulgated across the planet. The enemy wants to tear down the image of God, erect his own image, and bring hell to the world. If we ever want to see heaven come to earth as God intended, then the image of God must be restored in humanity.

4 - The Restoration of God's Image

The good news is that God Himself came to the earth as a human being, in the person of Jesus Christ, to restore His image in humanity. This is the message of the Bible - that the image of God that was distorted in Adam has been restored in Christ. And God is now actively working to heal the earth through this restored image.

Christ is "the image of the invisible God, the firstborn over all creation" (Colossians 1:15, NIV), the fullness of God in human form, and He came as a new federal head of the human race to overturn the destruction wrought by Adam's forfeiture of God's image. "For as in Adam all die, even so in Christ shall all be made alive" (1 Corinthians 15:22, KJV). Christ came to seek and to save that which was lost.

We now, as believers in Christ, are actively being transformed and conformed to His image, and we are reclaiming our right to rule as God's ambassadors in the earth. "For whom he did foreknow, he also did predestinate to be conformed to the image of his Son, that he might be the firstborn among many brethren" (Romans 8:29, KJV). We have taken off the old humanity and we have put on the new humanity, "which is renewed in knowledge after the image of him that created him" (Colossians 3:10, KJV).

The more we see Christ, the more we are transformed into His image and the more power we have to co-rule with God. For as we behold Him, we are being "transformed into the same image from one degree of glory to another" (2 Corinthians 3:18, ESV).

Christ and His Kingdom

The Dominion Mandate that was initially given to humanity is now being accomplished in Christ and His Kingdom. Jesus began His preaching ministry by saying, "Repent, for the kingdom of heaven has come near" (Matthew 4:17, NIV). And when His disciples asked Him to teach them how to pray, Jesus prayed to the Father, "your kingdom come, your will be done, on earth as it is in heaven" (Matthew 6:10, NIV). Jesus taught extensively about the Kingdom of God and manifested its power wherever He went.

What then is this Kingdom? The Kingdom of God refers to the "King's domain" - the "territory" that is actively being submitted to the rulership of Christ. It is the government of God, and this government will continue to advance until all competing powers eventually capitulate and surrender to His rule:

> "For unto us a child is born, unto us a son is given: and the government shall be upon his shoulder: and his name shall be called Wonderful, Counsellor, The mighty God, The everlasting Father, The Prince of Peace. Of the increase of his government and peace there shall be no end, upon the throne of David, and upon his kingdom, to order it, and to establish it with judgment and with justice from henceforth even for ever. The zeal of the Lord of hosts will perform this" (Isaiah 9:6-7, KJV).

> "For the earth shall be filled with the knowledge of the glory of the Lord, as the waters cover the sea" (Habakkuk 2:14, KJV).

> "The Lord will be king over the whole earth. On that day there will be one Lord, and his name the only name" (Zechariah 14:9, NIV).

> "And the seventh angel sounded; and there were great voices in heaven, saying, The kingdoms of this world are become the kingdoms of our Lord, and of his Christ; and he shall reign for ever and ever" (Revelation 11:15, KJV).

The Kingdom of God - the rule of God - will ultimately fill the earth through Christ and those who live in Him. Because of the work of Christ, God has put all things in subjection to Him, and from God's perspective, this work is already accomplished. The end is a foregone conclusion. However, this finished work has not yet fully manifested tangibly. It is still unfolding and being "worked out" throughout God's creation.

This is where we come in. When we become believers, we are translated into this Kingdom, and we are invited to recognize our heavenly citizenship and union with Christ. We are invited to set our hearts and minds on things above and to seek first the Kingdom of God, knowing that everything we need will be provided by our "home government." We become God's ambassadors, representing Him and advancing His rule. We become the restored image of God in the earth.

As believers, we are invited to participate with God, to co-rule with Him, until the finished work of Christ is fully manifested, until His cosmos is fully reconciled back to Him. We do this with the full assurance that eventually, every knee will bow, and every tongue will confess that Christ is Lord. At some point, as the Scriptures have said, everything will be surrendered to Christ, and God will be all in all.

The Name of Jesus

We as believers co-rule with God in the name of Jesus, for "in him we live, and move, and have our being" (Acts 17:28, KJV). Everything we do, whether in word or deed, we "do it all in the name of the Lord Jesus, giving thanks to God the Father through him" (Colossians 3:17, NIV). The "name" of Jesus does not primarily refer to the sound of the name when it is spoken. It refers to His essence, His character, and His authority. To do something "in the name of Jesus" is to do it in His stead, with His blessing and empowerment.

When we invoke the name of Jesus, we are invoking His reputation and His power. Thus, for example, praying "in the name of Jesus" means to pray in His Person, directed and authorized by Him - to pray as led by His Spirit and to bring forth revelation that flows from being in His presence. Therefore, "in Jesus' name" is not simply a religious formula for ending prayers. It is about becoming one with Christ, allowing His Spirit to flow through us, and accurately representing Him.

Jesus said, "I am the vine; you are the branches. If you remain in me and I in you, you will bear much fruit; apart from me you can do nothing" (John 15:5, NIV). The branches only have life and vitality as long as they remain connected to the Vine. In the same way, our union with Christ is what gives us the power to co-rule with God. Apart from abiding in Him, we have no true authority. All must be done in His name.

5 - The Four Levels of Power

The restored image of God in Christ produces four levels of power within the believer:

1. The Right
2. The Might
3. Inner Strength to Fight
4. Governing Systems

We will discuss each in turn.

The Right

The first level of power is the right to rule. This power is the divine authority given to the believer, and it involves authorization and legitimacy. The "right" gives you the privilege and clearance to exercise the power that has been invested in you.

The Greek word associated with this level of power is "exousia," and it can refer to authority, conferred power, delegated empowerment, or the right to act. When Jesus said, "All power is given unto me in heaven and in earth" (Matthew 28:18, KJV), the word translated "power" in that statement is the Greek word "exousia." Jesus was saying that all authority had been given to Him.

The Might

If the "right" is the authority, then the "might" is the ability, and both are required in order to get the job done. Most law enforcement officers have both a badge and a gun. The badge represents the authority to exercise power, and the gun represents the ability to exercise that power - the capacity to use force if necessary. Possessing authority without ability makes one "all bark and no bite," while exercising ability without authority makes one a renegade.

The Greek word associated with this level of power is "dunamis," and it can refer to might, strength, physical power, or the ability to perform. It was this kind of power that Jesus was referring to when He said, "you will receive power when the Holy Spirit comes on you" (Acts 1:8, NIV). When the Holy Spirit comes upon a person, that person is empowered with God's supernatural ability to accomplish a task and make something happen. They become a force to be reckoned with.

Inner Strength to Fight

The third level of power is the inner strength to fight. Co-ruling with Christ and advancing His Kingdom in the earth requires an internal fortitude and stamina that empowers one to persevere, to overcome obstacles, and to endure hardness as a good soldier. This power affords the believer the motivation, energy, and grit to confront opposition and accomplish the purposes of God.

The Greek word associated with this level of power is "ischuó," and it can refer to strength, vigor, ability to prevail, or combative force. This kind of power is illustrated in the statement, "I can do all things through him who strengthens me" (Philippians 4:13, ESV). "I can do" is a translation of "ischuó" or inner strength.

Governing Systems

The final level of power is that of governing systems. This power refers to "dominion" - the ability to steadfastly dominate until the will of God comes to pass in fullness and completion. It involves sustained governance and the implementation of systems that will produce a desired result.

The Greek word associated with this level of power is "kratos," from a root word that means "to perfect" or "to complete." It refers to dominion, exerted power, or mighty deeds. The word "kratos" is used when the Apostle Paul says, "Finally, my brethren, be strong in the Lord, and in the power of his might" (Ephesians 6:10, KJV).

It will take all four levels of power to see the Kingdom of God fully manifest on earth as it is in heaven. However, we can only exercise this power to the degree to which we have been conformed to the image of God in Christ.

Part Two
Conformity To Christ

Conformity to Christ

6 - Becoming Like Christ

Since God is now ruling in the earth through His restored image in Christ, we co-rule with Him to the degree to which we have been conformed to the image of God in Christ. In other words, we exercise God's authority and influence in the world only insofar as we have become Christlike. The more we experience union with Christ and the more the Spirit of God transforms us, the more power we receive to manifest Christ and advance His Kingdom.

We as believers are called not just to learn about Christ through study and analysis but to experience and manifest Him in the world. In Scripture, we are called the Body of Christ, of which He is the head. This means that, as parts of Christ's Body, we are one with Him, and we give expression to His will. Our lives are not our own, for we have been "purchased" by God through the blood of Jesus Christ, and our new lives are now hidden within Christ.

We must actively seek to receive and experience this new life in Christ. The Apostle Paul writes, "Since, then, you have been raised with Christ, set your hearts on things above, where Christ is, seated at the right hand of God. Set your minds on things above, not on earthly things. For you died, and your life is now hidden with Christ in God. When Christ, who is your life, appears, then you also will appear with him in glory" (Colossians 3:1-4, NIV). We must set our hearts and minds on things above; we must focus our gaze on things pertaining to Christ and His Kingdom.

The goal of the believer's life is to become more and more like Christ - to gradually grow to manifest His nature, character, and power. We experience this progressive conformation (or transformation) by identification, imprinting, imitation, and impartation.

Identification

To manifest Christ, we must identify with Him. Here are several definitions of the word "identify" that will help to clarify our meaning:[3]

- "to feel a sense of unity (as of interests, purpose, or effect) and close emotional association : to engage in psychological identification"
- "to conceive as united (as in spirit, outlook, or principle)"
- "to cause to be or become identical"

The word "identify" can also mean "to recognize or establish as being a particular person or thing."[4] To identify with Christ means to recognize Christ for who He is and to assume His identity by faith in His redemptive work. We so closely associate ourselves with Christ that we consider ourselves one with Him. His life becomes our life. As the Apostle Paul said, "I am crucified with Christ: nevertheless I live; yet not I, but Christ liveth in me: and the life which I

---

[3] "Identify." *Merriam-Webster.com Dictionary*, Merriam-Webster, https://www.merriam-webster.com/dictionary/identify. Accessed 1 Apr. 2022.

[4] "Identify." Dictionary.com, https://www.dictionary.com/browse/identify. Accessed 1 Apr. 2022.

now live in the flesh I live by the faith of the Son of God, who loved me, and gave himself for me" (Galatians 2:20, KJV).

In the incarnation, Jesus, the image of the invisible God, identified with humanity. He experienced the weaknesses and limitations of our earthly frames, and He took upon Himself our pain, sickness, and suffering. God, in Jesus, identified with us to the degree that He experienced the violence of the cross on our behalf. He assumed our identity and became sin for us so that we might become the righteousness of God in Him.

Christ identified with us so that we could identify with Him and, in some sense, as Him. Identification, then, is a spiritual principle. As we identify with the death, burial, resurrection, ascension, and reign of Christ, we are liberated from our old nature, and we become partakers of the divine nature. It is through identification with Christ that we receive the power to co-rule with Christ.

Imprinting

However, before we can actively identify with Christ, we must first "imprint" on Him. In psychobiology, imprinting is "a form of learning in which a very young animal fixes its attention on the first object with which it has visual, auditory, or tactile experience and thereafter follows that object. In nature the object is almost invariably a parent."[5]

---

[5] Britannica, The Editors of Encyclopaedia. "imprinting". Encyclopedia Britannica, 9 Mar. 2012, https://www.britannica.com/topic/imprinting-learning-behaviour. Accessed 2 April 2022.

Through imprinting, many animals receive their sense of species identification. Many birds, for example, visually imprint on their parents and then identify with them for life.

In our context, we must "see" Christ so that we can identify with Him. We must have an experience with Him that causes us to align our identity with His. For this reason, we are "fixing our eyes on Jesus, the pioneer and perfecter of faith" (Hebrews 12:2, NIV), knowing that as we see Him, we "are being transformed into his image with ever-increasing glory" (2 Corinthians 3:18, NIV). When we spiritually perceive Christ through the eyes of faith, we come to better understand our identity in Him.

Imitation

It has often been said that "imitation is the sincerest form of flattery." When we hold someone in high regard, we tend to model ourselves after that person. In fact, imitation is a pervasive phenomenon within human relationships in general.

"Rene Girard, the founder of mimetic theory, discovered a simple yet powerful pattern detectable in all interpersonal relationships, claiming that 'imitation is the fundamental mechanism of human behavior.' In other words, we become and we behave like the people with whom we keep company."[6]

---

[6]Peterson, Eric E. "Imprinting with God: The Lifelong Dynamic of Baptism as a Lifestyle." *Renovaré*, Apr. 2018, renovare.org/articles/imprinting-with-god.

When attempting to learn a new art form, sport, musical instrument, or craft, a student will often diligently and intelligently imitate another practitioner who has mastered the desired skill. This "mimetic transmission" is akin to the art of making disciples. For the Christian believer, this involves imitating the master, Christ Jesus, and becoming progressively more like Him.

We must learn to imitate Christ in the way He thinks, speaks, and acts so that we can be more conformed to His image. We are therefore instructed to "be imitators of God, as beloved children. And walk in love, as Christ loved us and gave himself up for us, a fragrant offering and sacrifice to God" (Ephesians 5:1-2, ESV). We are also encouraged to follow the example of godly leaders. For example, the Apostle Paul encourages the Philippian church to "join in imitating me, and keep your eyes on those who walk according to the example you have in us" (Philippians 3:17, ESV). Through imitation of God and divinely appointed leaders, we will experience greater conformity to Christ.

Impartation

Impartation is the transference of gifts from one person to another through the laying on of hands or other means. It involves the ability to give others that which God has allocated for them, and it rapidly accelerates spiritual growth. By receiving impartation, believers can experience a "quantum leap" in their spiritual journey as they learn from the Spirit of God in those with decades of experience. Ideally, growth by impartation should be a reality experienced by every single believer.

Impartation is often related to "transfer of spirits." After Moses commissioned Joshua, his successor, to lead the children of Israel, it was said that "Joshua the son of Nun was full of the spirit of wisdom, for Moses had laid his hands on him" (Deuteronomy 34:9, ESV). Moses imparted a spirit of wisdom to Joshua so that he could lead the people effectively. Similarly, the prophet Elisha, the protege of Elijah, received a "double portion" of Elijah's spirit.

Also related to the idea of impartation are the roles of mentors, coaches, fathers, and mothers. A mentor is someone who shares their knowledge, skills, and/or experience to help a mentee develop and grow. A coach is someone who provides guidance to another person with regard to that person's goals and helps that person reach their full potential. A father or mother does both.

7 - The Five Laws of the Cross

If we are to effectively co-rule with Christ, then we must first be conformed to Christ. This involves identifying with Him by daily experiencing His death, burial, resurrection, ascension, and reign. These are what we call the "Five Laws of the Cross." They are not simply tenants of doctrine that we intellectually ascribe to, nor are they simply historical events that we reflect back upon. They are eternal, living, spiritual laws, and as such, they have the capacity to govern our reality and our lived experience. These spiritual laws are present realities - spiritual dimensions that we can enter into and experience here and now. Only in this way will we be conformed to Christ, and only in this way will we receive the power to co-rule with Him.

For example, it is not enough simply to intellectually affirm our belief in the death of Christ on the cross. This is good, but it does little by way of transformation. If we want to be transformed by the death of Christ, then we must <u>experience</u> the death of Christ in realtime, as if it were really (spiritually) happening to us in the present moment. We must use our faith to identify with the crucified Christ such that His experience becomes our experience. We must become one with the death of Christ. When this happens, the death of Christ, as a spiritual law, will begin to operate within us, freeing us from the sin nature and everything else that is harming us; and we will reap the tangible benefits of Christ's sacrifice in our real lives.

At our church, Embassy Covenant Church International, we have crafted five pieces of "Kingdom legislation" to reflect these Five Laws of the Cross:

1. The Substitutionary Death and Emancipation Act
2. The Substitutionary Burial and Purification Act
3. The Substitutionary Resurrection and New Life Act
4. The Substitutionary Ascension and Spiritual Gifts Act
5. The Substitutionary Reign and Power Act

Each of these five acts articulates an aspect of what Christ accomplished on our behalf and what we have access to as a result. The next five subsections communicate the spirit of these five acts, and as previously stated, they correspond to the Five Laws of the Cross. (Some modifications and additions have been included for the sake of the book format. If you wish to see the pieces of legislation in their original formats, please see Appendix A. Additionally, Part 3 of this book will provide you with many helpful, practical tools that you can use to begin applying these spiritual laws in your own life.)

This is the path to transformation. This is the heart of conformity to Christ. And this is the way to co-rulership with Him. I personally invite you to experience the death, burial, resurrection, ascension, and reign of Christ for yourself, and I am confident that when you do, you will never be the same again.

Substitutionary Death and Emancipation

The substitutionary death of our Lord Jesus Christ was a legal act of divine judgment against sin, the carnal nature, the demonic kingdom, and the spirit of the world. The result of this substitutionary sacrifice was the emancipation of humanity from all powers antithetical to the Kingdom of God. Therefore, all humanity is invited to personally identify with and experience the liberating power of the death of Jesus Christ - a power that will free individuals, families, communities, and nations.

Human beings were created in the image of God and given a unique charge to govern the earth in God's stead, but Adam's rebellion tragically plunged all humanity into bondage. Fallen humanity was made subject to sin, the carnal nature, the demonic kingdom, and the spirit of the world - resulting in pain, suffering, violence, injustice, sickness, and death. In that fallen state, we were hopelessly unable to remedy our own condition.

God the Father demonstrated His infinite love, power, and wisdom by sending His only Son, Jesus Christ, to die on the cross as a representative of all humanity. The innocent was offered on behalf of the guilty, and this substitutionary sacrifice satisfied the righteous demands of God's justice and forever judged sin, the carnal nature, the demonic kingdom, and the spirit of the world - legally liberating humanity from these powers. Christ "forgave us all our sins, having canceled the charge of our legal indebtedness, which stood against us and condemned us; he has taken it away, nailing it to the cross. And having disarmed the powers and authorities, he made a public spectacle of them, triumphing over them by the cross" (Colossians 2:13b-15, NIV).

We manifest the tangible benefits of the death of Christ by believing, receiving, experiencing, and expressing this truth in the earth. As the Apostle Paul wrote, "I have been crucified with Christ and I no longer live, but Christ lives in me. The life I now live in the body, I live by faith in the Son of God, who loved me and gave himself for me" (Galatians 2:20, NIV). We must choose to carry our cross daily, reckon ourselves dead to sin, and allow the death of Christ to work within us, nullifying that which destroys. We activate the death of Christ by receiving it as a divine decree, confessing it, meditating on it, declaring it, and proclaiming/applying it to ourselves and to the world. May we say with the Apostle Paul, "the world has been crucified to me, and I to the world" (Galatians 6:14b, NIV). And may we be crucified to *everything* that hinders us from complete union with Christ.

Individuals, families, communities, and nations will benefit from this spiritual law by identifying with Christ and partaking of this grace. "For if we have been united with him in a death like his, we shall certainly be united with him in a resurrection like his" (Romans 6:5, ESV). By activating this power, humanity will experience unprecedented freedom.

Substitutionary Burial and Purification

The substitutionary burial of our Lord Jesus Christ was the effectual "putting away" of all human sin, resulting in the deliverance and complete purification of humanity.

Therefore, all believers are invited to personally identify with and experience the purifying power of the burial of Jesus Christ - a power that brings complete freedom from all forms of bondage and cleanses us from all unrighteousness.

After His death on the cross, Jesus Christ was buried on behalf of all humanity, and through this representative burial, He separated us from all sin, bondage, and corruption. In the burial of Christ, the record of sin was completely expunged and removed from us - as far as the east is from the west. It was buried in the burial of Christ, for God has said, "Their sins and lawless acts I will remember no more" (Hebrews 10:17, NIV). This burial also removed all negative influences, effects, stains, and structures within us that resulted from our prior condition. They were dismantled, destroyed, and tossed into a sea of forgetfulness.

Through the burial of Christ, God has purged us, washed us, and cleansed us from all unrighteousness, and He has legally liberated us from all demonic presence and power. Because of this burial, we are completely separated from the carnal nature, completely delivered from the bondage of the enemy, and completely purified from all corruption. We have a clean slate and a clear conscience, and no charges can be brought against us.

We manifest the tangible benefits of the burial of Christ by believing, receiving, experiencing, and expressing this truth in the earth. The Apostle John wrote, "Dear friends, now we are children of God, and what we will be has not yet been made known. But we know that when Christ appears, we shall be like him, for we shall see him as he is. All who have this hope in him purify themselves, just as he is pure" (1 John 3:2-3, NIV). As believers, we are invited to participate in sanctification - the purification associated with the burial of Christ. We activate the power of this burial by receiving it as a divine decree, confessing it, meditating on it, declaring it, and proclaiming/applying it to ourselves and to the world.

Individuals, families, communities, and nations will benefit from this spiritual law by identifying with Christ and partaking of this grace. "Blessed are the pure in heart, for they will see God" (Matthew 5:8, NIV). By activating this power, humanity will be redeemed from every lawless deed and purified as God's "own special people, zealous for good works" (Titus 2:14, NKJV).

Substitutionary Resurrection and New Life

The substitutionary resurrection of our Lord Jesus Christ was the conclusive and incontestable triumph of God over death, hell, and the grave. This triumph made divine life available to humanity, and all believers are invited to personally identify with and experience this new life associated with the resurrection of Jesus Christ - a life that makes us partakers of the divine nature.

Jesus Christ rose from the dead on behalf of all humanity, and through this representative resurrection, He forever conquered death, hell, and the grave. "And having disarmed the powers and authorities, he made a public spectacle of them, triumphing over them by the cross" (Colossians 2:15, NIV). Because of the resurrection of Christ, we too have triumphed over these powers, and we are subject to them no longer. "For the wages of sin is death; but the gift of God is eternal life through Jesus Christ our Lord" (Romans 6:23, KJV). Since we were united with Christ in His death, we were also united with Him in His resurrection. We are born from above, and we have been made partakers of the divine nature. Because of His resurrection, we live under an open heaven, and we have access to the nature, character, and Spirit of God.

We manifest the tangible benefits of the resurrection of Christ by believing, receiving, experiencing, and expressing this truth in the earth. "We were buried therefore with him by baptism into death, in order that, just as Christ was raised from the dead by the glory of the Father, we too might walk in newness of life" (Romans 6:4, ESV). As believers, we are invited to participate in the new life of Christ - to "put on Christ" and allow Him to live through us. Through the resurrection of Christ, we have access to the manifold grace of God and the inexhaustible riches of Christ. This new life (and inheritance) begins now and continues throughout eternity. We activate the power of this resurrection by receiving it as a divine decree, confessing it, meditating on it, declaring it, and proclaiming/applying it to ourselves and to the world.

When we embrace our oneness with the resurrected Christ, we are edified by our communion with Him, and we open the gateway to transformational experiences in Him. When we identify with the resurrection of Christ, we have access to the "spiritual blessings" in "heavenly realms" that the Apostle Paul wrote about (see Ephesians 1:3). Truly, within Christ, there are many spiritual "dimensions" or "places" we can visit as believers. There are entire worlds characterized by various aspects of the divine nature: love, joy, peace, patience, kindness, goodness, faith, gentleness, self-control, divine counsel, justice, zeal, holiness, truth, mercy, obedience, hope, generosity, etc. When we believe, we can experience "dimensional travel" to these spiritual realms, and we can be transformed by the nature of Christ Himself.

Individuals, families, communities, and nations will benefit from this spiritual law by identifying with Christ and partaking of this grace. "Praise be to the God and Father of our Lord Jesus Christ! In his great mercy he has given us new birth into a living hope through the resurrection of Jesus Christ from the dead, and into an inheritance that can never perish, spoil or fade" (1 Peter 1:3-4a, NIV). By activating this power, humanity will triumph over death, hell, and the grave, and we will manifest the life of Christ in the earth. Only those who walk in the power of Christ's resurrection are given the authority to co-rule with Him.

Substitutionary Ascension and Spiritual Gifts

The substitutionary ascension of our Lord Jesus Christ was the unconditional acceptance of humanity in Christ, resulting in spiritual gifts and mantles given to humanity. All believers are invited to personally identify with and experience this ascension, with all its associated affirmation, glorification, and grace.

After His death, burial, and resurrection, Jesus ascended into heaven on our behalf and was seated at the right hand of the Father, far above all principality and power and every name that is named. He was completely accepted and embraced, and all things were put under his feet. As a glorified man with a glorified human nature, Christ Jesus represents all humanity before God, and in Him, we are accepted in the beloved and seated at the right hand of God. We are citizens of the Kingdom of God, and our spiritual residence is in heaven. From this position of authority, Christ also gave gifts to humanity, including the fivefold ministry gifts, the gifts of the Spirit, callings, anointings, assignments, and mantles - for the profit of the Church and the human race.

We manifest the tangible benefits of the ascension of Christ by believing, receiving, experiencing, and expressing this truth in the earth. "Since, then, you have been raised with Christ, set your hearts on things above, where Christ is, seated at the right hand of God. Set your minds on things above, not on earthly things. For you died, and your life is now hidden with Christ in God" (Colossians 3:1-3, NIV). Because of Christ's ascension, we can fully embrace our acceptance in God; and by faith, we can receive every spiritual gift that He has allocated for us, knowing that "we have different gifts, according to the grace given to each of us" (Romans 12:6a, NIV). We activate the power of this ascension by receiving it as a divine decree, confessing it, meditating on it, declaring it, and proclaiming/applying it to ourselves and to the world.

When we identify with the ascension of Christ, we are clothed with power from on high for service in the Kingdom of God, and we have access to powerful supernatural experiences in Christ. We have access to the armor of God, spiritual weapons of warfare, the offices of Christ, the gifts of Christ, and the mantles of Christ. For example, someone could receive the office of the prophet or a word of wisdom or the grace to be a father - whatever God has determined for that individual. By the grace of God, may we fully tap into everything that He has stored up for us in heavenly places - that we may know the riches of His glorious inheritance.

Individuals, families, communities, and nations will benefit from this spiritual law by identifying with Christ and partaking of this grace. Gifts from heaven, such as the fivefold ministry gifts (apostle, prophet, evangelist, pastor, teacher), will bless the earth monumentally on behalf of Christ. By activating the power of Christ's ascension, humanity will walk in tremendous acceptance and spiritual empowerment.

Substitutionary Reign and Power

The substitutionary reign of our Lord Jesus Christ made us co-rulers with Christ, and it gave power and authority to humanity in Christ. All believers are invited to personally identify with and experience this reign so that we can be fully equipped and empowered to establish the Kingdom of God in the earth. Those who identify with the rule of Christ will testify of His life and Lordship to their generation, "for if, by the trespass of the one man, death reigned through that one man, how much more will those who receive God's abundant provision of grace and of the gift of righteousness reign in life through the one man, Jesus Christ!"
(Romans 5:17, NIV).

When Jesus ascended, the Father "seated him at his right hand in the heavenly realms, far above all rule and authority, power and dominion, and every name that is invoked, not only in the present age but also in the one to come. And God placed all things under his feet and appointed him to be head over everything for the church, which is his body, the fullness of him who fills everything in every way" (Ephesians 1:20b-23, NIV). And because we were in Christ when He ascended, "God raised us up with Christ and seated us with him in the heavenly realms in Christ Jesus" (Ephesians 2:6, NIV). In Him, we are ruling and reigning in majesty, and we have been given authority over all the power of the enemy. We are co-heirs with Christ who will inherit all things, and we are exercising governance and dominion for the glory of God - each of us according to our own measure of rule. This co-rulership begins in this life and continues throughout the ages.

We manifest the tangible benefits of the reign of Christ by believing, receiving, experiencing, and expressing this truth in the earth. Christ is ruling and reigning from the heavens, and by faith, we are reigning with Him, for in Him we live and move and have our being. We have the opportunity to seek God's counsel and hear His decrees so that we can manifest them in our world. Through co-rulership with Christ, we are partnering to bring God's Kingdom agenda to pass. We activate the power of this reign by receiving it as a divine decree, confessing it, meditating on it, declaring it, and proclaiming/applying it to ourselves and to the world.

Individuals, families, communities, and nations will benefit from this spiritual law by identifying with Christ and partaking of this grace. Through the reign of God's people in Christ, the Kingdom of God will come, and the will of God will be done on earth as it is in heaven. Christ will reign until all creation is made subject to Him and until all the kingdoms of the world have become the Kingdom of God; and His people will reign with Him forever and ever. By activating the power of Christ's reign, humanity will experience the limitless benefits associated with being under the rule of Christ.

A Daily Practice

It is important to remember that we must *daily* experience the death, burial, resurrection, ascension, and reign of Christ. Although the work is finished from God's perspective, we must consistently apply it to our lives in order to experience the benefits of that work. Every single day, we must die with Christ, be buried with Christ, rise with Christ, ascend with Christ, and reign with Christ. This is a perpetual practice - a way of life.

8 - Living and Ruling in Christ

When we consistently identify with the death, burial, resurrection, ascension, and reign of Christ, we are empowered to live and rule in Christ. "For in him we live and move and have our being" (Acts 17:28a, NIV). In fact, to the degree to which we are conformed to Christ, we begin to function as Christ in this present world, for we are parts of His Body. As His image in the earth, and as partakers of the divine nature, we are an extension of Him. In this sense, then, we can truly say, "I am one with Christ" or even, in a qualified sense, "I am Christ."

Jesus prayed this very prayer before He went to the cross. He prayed that we would be one with Him and that we would be one with one another:

> "My prayer is not for them alone. I pray also for those who will believe in me through their message, that all of them may be one, Father, just as you are in me and I am in you. May they also be in us so that the world may believe that you have sent me. I have given them the glory that you gave me, that they may be one as we are one—I in them and you in me—so that they may be brought to complete unity. Then the world will know that you sent me and have loved them even as you have loved me" (John 17:20-23, NIV).

What an astounding prayer! Just as Christ is one with the Father, so we can be one with Christ. The *telos* (ultimate end) of our existence is union with Christ. Such intimacy and such power! And it is only by virtue of our union with Christ that we have any power or authority to co-rule with Him. When we experience oneness with Christ, we become conscious of our ability to rule as Christ in the earth, for "as He is, so are we in this world" (1 John 4:17b, NKJV).

Partnering with Holy Spirit

I'm sure by now you may be wondering, "How does a person see or have an experience with Christ Jesus? Since everything that is needed to co-rule is contingent upon identifying with Him, what must we do?" The answer to this trillion dollar question is simple yet profound. The short answer is to partner with Holy Spirit. As a matter of fact, partnering with Holy Spirit is the only means by which we are able to use the tools of the trade, activate the gifts of the Spirit, and be conformed into the image of God. The long answer involves learning to be led by Holy Spirit in all we do.

Again, Jesus commanded His disciples to both receive and partner with Holy Spirit as the only means of being conformed into His image and satisfying the criteria necessary for co-ruling. Holy Spirit's responsibility and work in the believer's life is comprehensive, to say the least. By Him, believers are able to receive a personal, guided tour of the Kingdom of God and the spirit world. He is also responsible for showing us things to come, comforting us, and providing us with a supernatural education in the things of God. His most important work in the lives of believers is to restore the image of God in them by revealing Christ to them. Consider what Jesus says in the following two passages:

> "I have much more to say to you, more than you can now bear. But when he, the Spirit of truth, comes, he will guide you into all the truth. He will not speak on his own; he will speak only what he hears, and he will tell you what is yet to come. He will glorify me because it is from me that he will receive what he will make known to you. All that belongs to the Father is mine. That is why I said the Spirit will receive from me what he will make known to you" (John 16:12-15, NIV).

> "And I will ask the Father, and he will give you another advocate to help you and be with you forever—the Spirit of truth. The world cannot accept him, because it neither sees him nor knows him. But you know him, for he lives with you and will be in you. I will not leave you as orphans; I will come to you. Before long, the world will not see me anymore, but you will see me. Because I live, you also will live. On that day you will realize that I am in my Father, and you are in me, and I am in you. Whoever has my commands and keeps them is the one who loves me. The one who loves me will be loved by my Father, and I too will love them and show myself to them." Then Judas (not Judas Iscariot) said, "But, Lord, why do you

intend to show yourself to us and not to the world?" Jesus replied, "Anyone who loves me will obey my teaching. My Father will love them, and we will come to them and make our home with them. Anyone who does not love me will not obey my teaching. These words you hear are not my own; they belong to the Father who sent me. All this I have spoken while still with you. But the Advocate, the Holy Spirit, whom the Father will send in my name, will teach you all things and will remind you of everything I have said to you" (John 14:16-26, NIV).

Learning to partner with Holy Spirit is the only means we have of seeing and experiencing Christ. My present practice after 34 years of pastoral ministry is to ask Holy Spirit to give me experiences with Christ in whatever area I need Him to activate in me.

On one occasion, I needed the Prophet Christ Jesus to manifest in me to speak to a person's destiny. I simply asked Holy Spirit to reveal what Christ said or did for the person I was ministering to, and suddenly, Holy Spirit allowed me to hear and see what Christ was saying and doing. Thereafter, I ministered that aspect of Christ to the person. I told this particular individual that I saw him operating in what some call the five-fold ministry, pastoring a local church. He immediately rejected the prophecy because he was presently practicing a sinful lifestyle. He boldly said to my face that I had missed God on this one. Of course, I was not shaken or discouraged by his response because Holy Spirit had clearly revealed Christ's work in his life in me and to me. (Notice I said that Holy Spirit revealed Christ's work in his life not just *to me* but *in me*. Whatever He reveals becomes an internal experience that can be seen, heard, and felt.) At the time of this writing, the person I'm referencing has been pastoring for over 10 years. God did in that person's life exactly what He showed me by His Holy Spirit.

If another situation causes for Christ Jesus the Judge to be activated, then we should ask Holy Spirit to reveal Christ Jesus the Judge in us. We must ask Holy Spirit to reveal in us whatever part of Christ is needed to heal or bless every situation we are facing. Anyone who partners with Holy Spirit in this way shall be empowered to know His decrees and execute His Will in the earth.

Measure of Rule

When we identify with Christ and we are conformed to His image, we have power to co-rule with Him. However, we must also give an important caveat with regard to "measure of rule." Every believer, by the grace of God, has been given a certain "territory" to govern. We must learn to govern our territory well, and we must also be careful not to go beyond our "measure" into someone else's territory. The Apostle Paul described the community of believers as many parts of one body, of which Christ is the head. Each part is valuable, each part has a specific function, and each part is dependent on the whole. Just as the human body is governed by various systems and parts working together, so it must be in the Body of Christ.

In his second letter to the church in Corinth, Paul speaks of his measure of rule:

> But we will not boast of things without our measure, but according to the measure of the rule which God hath distributed to us, a measure to reach even unto you. For we stretch not ourselves beyond our measure, as though we reached not unto you: for we are come as far as to you also in preaching the gospel of Christ: Not boasting of things without our measure, that is, of other men's labours; but having hope, when your faith is increased, that we shall be enlarged by you according to our rule abundantly, To preach the gospel in the regions beyond you, and not to boast in another man's line of things made ready to our hand. But he that glorieth, let him glory in the Lord. For not he that commendeth himself is approved, but whom the Lord commendeth (2 Corinthians 10:13-18, KJV).

Paul recognized that God had given him a measure of rule - a sphere of governance that he was responsible for - and that others had done work in their own respective territories. Paul did hope to expand his territory and reach more people with the Good News of Jesus Christ, but he would not claim another man's labors as his own.

Because God has gifted us in different ways, we can benefit greatly from team ministry - partnering together in our various capacities to edify the Body of Christ and enhance the work of the Kingdom. For example, when the fivefold gifts (apostle, prophet, evangelist, pastor, teacher) function together according to the divine pattern, the power of the overall ministry is exponentially increased.

Our Promised Land

Many of us are familiar with the story of Moses - how God used him to deliver the children of Israel from Egyptian bondage. We remember the enslavement of God's people, the plagues upon Egypt, the first Passover, the parting of the Red Sea, the wandering in the wilderness, and eventually - through Moses's successor - the conquering of the Promised Land.

This epic story has resonated with humanity for thousands of years, but when we look closely, we can also clearly see within it the "types and shadows" that prefigure our salvation journey through Christ Jesus. Looking back at this story through the lens of Christ, we can understand it not just historically, but allegorically and spiritually, as well. Therefore...

Egyptian bondage	=	Bondage to sin
Blood on the doorposts (Passover)	=	Redemption by the blood of Jesus
Walking through the Red Sea	=	Baptism into Christ

If we extend the allegory, what then is our Promised Land as believers in Christ? Just as Joshua and the children of

Israel took territory and conquered the land that God had allocated to them, we have an opportunity as believers to take the "spiritual territory" that God has given to us. We must ask ourselves:

- How much of Christ am I able to possess?
- How much of me is Christ actively ruling?
- How much of my assigned "measure of rule" is experiencing the will of God?
- Is the Kingdom of God coming to my life, my family, and my community?

God has predetermined the spiritual territory that we are meant to rule, and we must actively exercise our power and authority to fully take and govern that territory for the Kingdom of God.

Ruling with Christ - Now to Eternity

Our co-rulership with Christ begins now and extends into eternity. With this in mind, we must be careful to avoid two polar extremes:

- The belief that because Christ will eventually come again, our efforts in this present world are feeble or even futile - that what we do really doesn't matter because only the return of Christ will set things right. We are just "on our way to heaven and so glad."
- The belief that we can fully manifest the Kingdom of God on this earth prior to the return of Christ - that the church can govern so effectively that we

essentially usher in the new heavens and new earth before the Second Coming.

We must plant our feet somewhere in the middle of these two extremes. The truth is that our co-rulership with Christ really does start right now and that we have power to bring heaven to earth in many significant ways. We can begin to manifest the Kingdom of God on this earth now. However, we are also cognizant of the fact that Christ is returning and that the earth will not be fully restored without His Second Coming. Our co-rulership with Christ now is an active part of God's process of restoration - a process that will culminate with the return of Christ.

9 - Miracles: Two Case Studies

Partnering with Holy Spirit to co-rule with Christ leads to miraculous results in the lives of believers. Here are two real-life examples that I will offer as case studies:

Case #1: Prophetic Alignment

During the early 2000's, I was conducting a somewhat routine prophetic destiny session with one of the members of our church. A prophetic destiny session is an appointed time when apostles and prophets join together to personally speak into the lives of individuals. On this occasion, the Word of the Lord came to me regarding a particular young lady's destiny. I saw her working in the field of news broadcasting in the Washington, D.C. area and birthing three children. At the time, she was living in Detroit, working in a different field, without any children.

The Word of the Lord confirmed this young lady's childhood aspiration of having a career in news broadcasting. She believed the Word of the Lord to the degree that she convinced her husband to move to Washington, D.C. As of this writing, she has lived in the Washington, D.C. area for several years, working for Fox News and MSNBC, and she is currently an executive at CNN. The Lord also miraculously blessed her and her husband with three beautiful children.

Case #2: Physical Healing

In 2021, a middle-aged woman scheduled a meeting with me as a result of hearing about our ministry's focus on redemptive justice and co-rulership. She was suffering from plantar fasciitis, scoliosis, insomnia, and multiple miscarriages. (Plantar fasciitis is "inflammation of the dense fibrous band of tissue of the sole of the foot that is marked especially by heel or arch pain."[7] This daughter of the Kingdom explained to me how this disease required her to wear special shoes and braces at times.)

After I completed my customary interview and investigative work with her, I asked Holy Spirit to reveal to me the decree of the Lord for her situation. I heard God grant her joy in the form of a decree from His Heavenly Council. Thereafter, I spent some time meditating on the decree, then began ministering the treatment to her spirit, soul, and body. After I began co-ruling and executing the Kingdom agenda, she was totally healed from all of these conditions. She no longer suffers from plantar fasciitis and insomnia, her chiropractor said her spine has straightened itself, and she is two months pregnant at the time of this writing.

All of this happened because God opened a portal of divine joy over her life by His decree. The joy of the Lord is God's celebration of His victory over everything, including plantar fasciitis, scoliosis, insomnia, and multiple miscarriages. As a result of displacing fear, brokenness, bad memories, toxic

---

[7] "Plantar fasciitis." Merriam-Webster.com Dictionary, Merriam-Webster, https://www.merriam-webster.com/dictionary/plantar%20fasciitis. Accessed 10 Aug. 2022.

spirit connections, etc. and ministering His joy or victory to her spirit, soul, and body, she was completely healed.

Profoundly Simple and Simply Profound

Each of these miraculous occurrences was preempted by asking Holy Spirit to give me a revelation or experience with what Christ had done in the person's life. It may appear as if I am over-simplifying a very profound thing. However, I've learned that everything in Christ is both profoundly simple and simply profound. Think about it: any kindergartner can look up, experience the Sun, and identify it by name. On the other hand, an astrophysicist can look up, experience the Sun, and provide an in-depth explanation of that same Sun. Therefore, it is not a stretch to conclude that our Sun is both profoundly simple and simply profound.

The same is true of the Son of God who provides life and light to all. He is simple enough for all to come and receive salvation by faith in Him, and He is profound to the degree that all who come are satisfied in Him because He is the express image of the invisible God. It is a simple thing to ask Holy Spirit to reveal Christ Jesus to us, but it is a profound thing to cultivate an in-depth relationship with Holy Spirit so that we might understand what is being revealed. I encourage every believer to receive the baptism of the Holy Spirit and begin training your human spirit to know and respond to Holy Spirit.

Consider what Paul the Apostle says:

> For those who are led by the Spirit of God are the children of God. The Spirit you received does not make you slaves, so that you live in fear again; rather, the Spirit you received brought about your adoption to sonship. And by him we cry, "Abba, Father." The Spirit himself testifies with our spirit that we are God's children. Now if we are children, then we are heirs—heirs of God and co-heirs with Christ, if indeed we share in his sufferings in order that we may also share in his glory (Romans 8:14-17, NIV).

Cultivating a relationship with the Spirit of God requires the believer to commit to four important things:

1. Becoming conscious of one's own human spirit.
2. Becoming conscious of Holy Spirit's promptings and impressions.
3. Growing in the knowledge of the written Word of God.
4. Practicing obedience to Holy Spirit and the written Word of God.

This subject will be discussed in great detail in our next book entitled, "The Human Blueprint."

The kinds of miracles described above will happen anytime a Kingdom portal is opened over a person's life by a divine decree. The Will of God can really come to pass in the earth regarding anything when people are familiar with what I call "the tools of the trade" and are trained in the art of co-ruling. I believe our Lord trained His disciples in this practice before He entrusted the Church to them. I also believe this is a huge part of the "Father's business" that Jesus was referencing at the age of twelve. Therefore, it is highly plausible that a well-trained team of apostles and prophets could also, through this same art of co-ruling, have a significant impact on our world for good.

In Part 3 of this book, we will provide insight into the "Heavenly Council" (where our governing work begins), and we will equip you with practical "tools of the trade" that you can use to begin co-ruling with Christ.

Part Three
The Heavenly Council

The Heavenly Council and Tools of the Trade

In this final section of the book, we will help you put co-rulership with Christ into practice. We will first discuss the reality and importance of the Heavenly Council (where our co-rulership begins) and then we will provide you with several "tools of the trade" that will help you manifest the will of God in the earth in tangible ways.

10 - The Heavenly Council

The Heavenly Council is the heavenly place from which God rules. The council is composed of angelic beings and some human beings, and its purpose is to govern the purpose of God and its fulfillment throughout the universe. The council accomplishes this task through legislation (enacting laws) and litigation (adjudicating cases). It is from this place that God issues divine decrees that shape reality and destiny.

Scriptural Support

The notion of a divine council may be new for some believers, so it will be helpful to provide some Scriptural support for this reality. The Scriptures reference the Heavenly Council in many places. Here are several good examples (emphasis mine):

> The heavens praise your wonders, Lord, your faithfulness too, in **the assembly of the**

holy ones. For who in the skies above can compare with the Lord? Who is like the Lord among the heavenly beings? In **the council of the holy ones** God is greatly feared; he is more awesome than all who surround him (Psalm 89:5-7, NIV).

God has taken his place in **the divine council**; in the midst of the gods he holds judgment (Psalm 82:1, ESV).

One day the members of **the heavenly court** came to present themselves before the Lord, and the Accuser, Satan, came with them (Job 1:6, NLT).

Micaiah continued, "Therefore hear the word of the Lord: I saw the Lord sitting on his throne with all the multitudes of heaven standing around him on his right and on his left" (1 Kings 22:19, NIV).

The sentence is by the decree of the watchers, the decision by the word of the holy ones, to the end that the living may know that the Most High rules the kingdom of men and gives it to whom he will and sets over it the lowliest of men (Daniel 4:17, ESV).

In these passages and others, the Bible affirms the existence of a divine council of heavenly beings that assist God by carrying out His judgments and directives.

Decrees (Scrolls)

From the Heavenly Council, God issues divine decrees. A decree is a "a formal and authoritative order, especially one having the force of law."[8] It can also be defined as a judicial decision, judgment, or order. In the realm of theology, a decree is "one of the eternal purposes of God, by which events are foreordained."[9] When God issues a decree, He is making a divine ruling on a particular matter.

For example, God decreed the vocation of the prophet Jeremiah before He was even born. When Jeremiah was still very young, God said to him, "Before I formed you in the womb I knew you, before you were born I set you apart; I appointed you as a prophet to the nations" (Jeremiah 1:5, NIV). In another place, David declares of God, "For you created my inmost being; you knit me together in my mother's womb. ... Your eyes saw my unformed body; all the days ordained for me were written in your book before one of them came to be" (Psalm 139:13,16, NIV).

God has made decisions about many things over which we have little to no control. The decrees of God contain the destinies of the following (and perhaps much more):

- Date of birth
- Date of death

---

[8] "Decree." Dictionary.com, https://www.dictionary.com/browse/decree. Accessed 1 Apr. 2022.
[9] Ibid.

- Gender
- Ethnicity
- Family
- Residence
- Gifts, talents, and calling
- Words
- Resources
- Sufferings
- Boundaries of nations
- Purposes of nations
- Moral law
- Laws of the physical universe

In Scripture, the decrees of God are sometimes symbolized by scrolls. The prophet Ezekiel received such a scroll from the Lord: "Then I looked, and I saw a hand stretched out to me. In it was a scroll, which he unrolled before me. On both sides of it were written words of lament and mourning and woe. And he said to me, 'Son of man, eat what is before you, eat this scroll; then go and speak to the people of Israel.' So I opened my mouth, and he gave me the scroll to eat" (Ezekiel 2:9-3:2, NIV). The prophet Ezekiel was instructed to eat the scroll that he received from the Lord. In other words, he was to consume the divine decree until it was part of him. He was to become one with the word of the Lord, and then he was to prophesy to the nation based on that word. The prophet Jeremiah also "ate" the words of the Lord (see Jeremiah 15:16). Similarly, John (the author of Revelation) was instructed to eat a heavenly scroll and was then instructed to continue his prophetic work (see Revelation 10:8-11).

Another example of a scroll as a divine decree can be found in the writings of the prophet Zechariah:

> I looked again, and there before me was a flying scroll. He asked me, "What do you see?" I answered, "I see a flying scroll, twenty cubits long and ten cubits wide." And he said to me, "This is the curse that is going out over the whole land; for according to what it says on one side, every thief will be banished, and according to what it says on the other, everyone who swears falsely will be banished. The Lord Almighty declares, 'I will send it out, and it will enter the house of the thief and the house of anyone who swears falsely by my name. It will remain in that house and destroy it completely, both its timbers and its stones'" (Zechariah 5:1-4, NIV).

In this case, the scroll was a divine judgment against thieves and false witnesses in the land. It would be sent out, enter houses, and destroy them.

"Cutting Realities" Based on Divine Decrees

In the English language, the suffix "cide" means "to cut" or "to kill." Therefore, homicide refers to the killing of another human being, suicide to the killing of oneself, and genocide to the killing of a people group. The same suffix "cide" can be found in the word "decide." Thus, the word "decide," in its etymology, means to "cut off." When we decide something, we are literally cutting off every possible alternative. We are "cutting a reality" in the universe - defining what will be and what will not be.

We must cut these realities based on the decrees of God - the divine rulings made by God at the Heavenly Council. We must declare what God has decreed until His reality manifests on the earth. The journey of life, with all its complex choices and possibilities, could be visualized as a multi-lane highway with many "alternate realities" splintering off from the main road, but when we align ourselves to God's foreordained purpose, we carve out a path that mirrors His trajectory for our lives.

The Courts of Heaven

Heaven's Court is the specific heavenly location in which cases are litigated and believers are privileged to submit prayer, petition, and intercession. In this place, God hears cases and renders verdicts as the sovereign Judge of the universe. The prophet Daniel describes the seating of the court in a heavenly vision:

> As I looked, thrones were set in place, and the Ancient of Days took his seat. His clothing was as white as snow; the hair of his head was white like wool. His throne was flaming with fire, and its wheels were all ablaze. A river of fire was flowing, coming out from before him. Thousands upon thousands attended him; ten thousand times ten thousand stood before him. The court was seated, and the books were opened (Daniel 7:9-10, NIV).

Have you ever noticed the many legal terms used throughout the Bible? The legal language in Scripture is prolific. Here are some examples:

- Law
- Justification
- Guilt
- Penalty
- Petition
- Throne
- Statutes
- Commandments
- Heaven's Court
- Adversary
- Judgments
- Advocate
- Confession
- Redemption
- Guilt
- Justice
- Bribe
- Mediation
- Witness
- Testimony
- Trial
- Complaint
- Restitution
- Order
- Examination
- Oath
- Promise
- Appeal

- Charge

- Conviction
- Counsel
- Crime
- Plea
- Prosecute
- Sentence
- Case
- Verdict
- Offense
- Evidence
- Accusation
- Contract language (bind, loose)

In many ways, God operates according to a governmental, legal framework - as evidenced by the abundance of legal terminology that is used in Scripture. Therefore, if we are to co-rule with Christ, we must familiarize ourselves with Heaven's Court and how it operates.

God often hears cases at Heaven's Court. In one place, God said to the nation of Israel, "I, even I, am he who blots out your transgressions, for my own sake, and remembers your sins no more. Review the past for me, let us argue the matter together; state the case for your innocence" (Isaiah 43:25-26, NIV). In this courtroom setting, God is willing to hear witnesses offer testimonies and arguments before He renders a verdict in the case.

In another significant example, the adversary was bringing a case against the high priest Joshua at Heaven's Court, but God, the angel of the Lord, and the prophet Zechariah all intervened. Zechariah was having a vision about the deliberations of this case in the spirit world, and he became an active participant in the proceedings. Consider how the story unfolded:

> Then he showed me Joshua the high priest standing before the angel of the Lord, and Satan standing at his right side to accuse him. The Lord said to Satan, "The Lord rebuke you, Satan! The Lord, who has chosen Jerusalem, rebuke you! Is not this man a burning stick snatched from the fire?" Now Joshua was dressed in filthy clothes as he stood before the angel. The angel said to those who were standing before him, "Take off his filthy clothes." Then he said to Joshua, "See, I have taken away your sin, and I will put fine garments on you." Then I said, "Put a clean turban on his head." So they put a clean turban on his head and clothed him, while the angel of the Lord stood by. The angel of the Lord gave this charge to Joshua: "This is what the Lord Almighty says: 'If you will walk in obedience to me and keep my requirements, then you will govern my house and have charge of my courts, and I will give you a place among these standing here. Listen, High Priest Joshua, you and your associates seated before you, who are men symbolic of things to come: I am going to bring my servant, the Branch. See, the stone I have set in front of Joshua! There are seven eyes on that one stone, and I will engrave an inscription on it,' says the Lord Almighty, 'and I will remove

the sin of this land in a single day. In that day each of you will invite your neighbor to sit under your vine and fig tree,' declares the Lord Almighty" (Zechariah 3:1-10, NIV).

In this powerful and insightful chapter, we are offered a window into the operations of Heaven's Court. The prophet Zechariah was not just <u>witnessing</u> the proceedings; he was <u>participating</u> in them. In this heavenly place, at the word of Zechariah, a clean turban was placed upon the head of the high priest, representing (along with the new, clean garments) the high priest's spiritual restoration. Though the adversary was bringing a case against Joshua, his prosecutorial arguments were ultimately overturned. God even said that Joshua could be given the privilege of participating in Heaven's Court if he obeyed God's commands.

As believers in Christ, we have been given a similar opportunity to begin operating in Heaven's Court. There are many situations in which our adversary has made cases against God's people, and we must learn how to address these cases and bring them before the just rule of God. We have been given power and authority to argue cases before God and receive His verdicts. This is legitimate spiritual work that has the potential to significantly impact the lives and destinies of individuals, communities, and even nations. And it's work that must be done.

The Ruling Church

The Church is God's government on the earth, and we have been given the authority to receive decrees from the

Heavenly Council and to declare, legislate, and adjudicate those decrees until they become manifested reality on this terra firma. We are the called out assembly of God, the citizens of the Kingdom, the ambassadors of heaven - and we are here to rule on heaven's behalf. We are here to ensure that the Kingdom of God comes and that His will is done on earth as it is in heaven. We are a powerful people, and we are here to transform the world.

Jesus highlights the authority given to the Church in the following passage:

> If your brother or sister sins, go and point out their fault, just between the two of you. If they listen to you, you have won them over. But if they will not listen, take one or two others along, so that 'every matter may be established by the testimony of two or three witnesses.' If they still refuse to listen, tell it to the church; and if they refuse to listen even to the church, treat them as you would a pagan or a tax collector. Truly I tell you, whatever you bind on earth will be bound in heaven, and whatever you loose on earth will be loosed in heaven. Again, truly I tell you that if two of you on earth agree about anything they ask for, it will be done for them by my Father in heaven. For where two or three gather in my name, there am I with them (Matthew 18:15-20, NIV).

The Church has been given the authority to hear cases and render verdicts based on the will of God. We have been given the power to "bind" (to restrict something from operating) and "loose" (to release something to operate). When we gather in His Name (His essence and character) and agree together in His Spirit, nothing is impossible. Heaven will back up what we declare.

The key is that we must hear the legitimate decrees of God from the Heavenly Council. Through the prophet Jeremiah, God addressed those who were declaring things that God had not decreed: "I did not send these prophets, yet they have run with their message; I did not speak to them, yet they have prophesied. But if they had stood in my council, they would have proclaimed my words to my people and would have turned them from their evil ways and from their evil deeds" (Jeremiah 23:21-22, NIV). We must stand in the council of God and hear His rulings if we are going to make legitimate, powerful declarations in His Name.

At the end of the day, the enemy doesn't care how much we quote Scripture or prophesy, as long as there is no Church that will actually bring the will of God into being. But when we begin to manifest the decrees of God in tangible ways, we become a threat to the kingdom of darkness. The next chapter will provide you with the practical tools that you need in order to bring the will of heaven to earth.

11 - Tools of the Trade

Imagine that you are beginning a DIY construction project at home, and you retrieve your toolbox from the garage. You open the toolbox, and you see a hammer, a screwdriver, a wrench, pliers, and several other items - each with a specific design and purpose. The more familiar you are with each tool and how/when to use it, the more effective you will be in completing your project successfully. In a similar way, the more you familiarize yourself with the "tools of the trade" contained in this chapter, and the more you put them into practice, the more effective you will be at bringing the will of God to the earth. This chapter contains 17 spiritual tools that will equip you to co-rule with Christ - to manifest the decrees that you receive from the Heavenly Council.

In order to ground the discussion in a real-life situation, let's describe a hypothetical case:

> Let's say "Joe" is a single 35-year-old African American man. Joe experienced a childhood trauma in elementary school that caused him to suppress his authentic emotions. He didn't know how to properly categorize what happened to him, so he shut down. Many internal issues were left unaddressed over the years, and as a result, he developed an anxiety disorder in his early twenties. This disorder prevented him from being successful in many ways, and to this day, Joe has not been able to fully manifest the dream God has for his life. He often feels a sense of frustration and anger, and

he grapples with bouts of depression - as well as pain in his physical body. Sometimes, in moments of intense frustration, he curses his life.

With this case in mind, let's explore the tools of the trade!

1. Decree

This is where it all begins. As we stated in the last chapter, God issues divine decrees from the Heavenly Council. A decree is a "a formal and authoritative order, especially one having the force of law."[10] It can also be defined as a judicial decision, judgment, or order. In the realm of theology, a decree is "one of the eternal purposes of God, by which events are foreordained."[11]

Stated another way, a decree is a divine edict or spiritual law that opens a heavenly "portal" over a human situation. Every time Holy Spirit reveals to a person what He has said or done on a matter, God is trying to bring heaven to earth. I am persuaded that every decree executed by a co-ruler has the potential to fundamentally transform any human condition.

In the early 90's, I was pastoring a small church in the city of Battle Creek, Michigan when I heard Jesus command me by decree to sell our small building with a capacity of 250 people and build a new facility on the city's north side. He

---

[10] "Decree." Dictionary.com, https://www.dictionary.com/browse/decree. Accessed 1 Apr. 2022.
[11] Ibid.

also said our ministry would double in size if I obeyed His decree. Thereafter, I communicated this message to our leaders, who were rightfully skeptical at such a saying. However, they capitulated, and we immediately sold our building. At that point in time, I was absolutely inexperienced in the processes associated with building anything. This was a walk of faith, to say the least.

While preparing to begin the project, we leased a large church building for our congregation to maintain worship services in the interim period. And just as God promised by His decree, the church doubled in its membership while we were leasing this space; and by the grace of God, we completed construction on our new, spacious edifice approximately two years from the time we started the project.

When God issues a decree, He is making a divine ruling on a particular matter. God speaks with sovereign authority, and His voice is the voice of command. "For the word of a king is authoritative and powerful, and who will say to him, 'What are you doing?'" (Ecclesiastes 8:4, AMP). The first step in the process of active co-rulership is to accurately discern and receive what God has decreed. This involves spending dedicated time in the presence of the Lord and being familiar with the truth contained in His Word.

Practical Example:

Remember Joe's case from earlier. Let's say that you as the minister/intercessor bring Joe's case before the throne of God at the Heavenly Council. You have "picked up" Joe in your spirit -

empathizing with his present state - and you are carrying him to God. On Joe's behalf, you receive what God decrees in his case - the wisdom of God's predetermined counsel for Joe. And let's say that decree is the PEACE of God. Representing Joe before God, you receive that decree in the Spirit.

Once you know and receive what God has decreed, you can utilize all the "tools of the trade" that follow in order to bring that decree to pass in Joe's life.

2. Confession

After we hear God's divine decree, our next step is to confess what He has decreed. To confess, in this context, means to say the same thing openly, without reservation. When we make a confession, we are formally acknowledging and agreeing with what God has said - whether regarding our sin, the tenets of our faith, or God's specific will in a situation. Our confession aligns us to God's decree.

The Apostle Paul tells Timothy to "fight the good fight of the faith. Take hold of the eternal life to which you were called when you made your good confession in the presence of many witnesses" (1 Timothy 6:12, NIV). Whether public or private, open confession before God helps us to come into agreement with His truth and His reality.

Practical Example:

Back to Joe's case. You know that God has decreed His peace, and you have received that divine decree in your spirit. The next step is to openly confess and agree with what God has decreed.

You might say something like, "Lord, thank you for your decree of peace for Joe. I fully receive that decree in my spirit. I am in full agreement with it, and it shall come to pass, in Jesus' mighty name."

3. Meditation

Next, we must meditate on the divine decree. The biblical definition of "meditation" is generally "to mutter, moan, utter, muse, or speak quietly." Meditation is the act of musing or focusing one's thoughts on a specific subject. It consists of reflective thinking or contemplation, usually for the purpose of becoming one with the Word. When you meditate on God's decree, you are allowing yourself to become one with that decree.

Thomas Brooks, a seventeenth-century church leader, said it this way:

> Remember that it is not hasty reading but serious meditation on holy and heavenly truths, that makes them prove sweet and profitable to the soul. It is not the mere touching of the flower by the bee that gathers honey, but her abiding for a time on the flower that draws out the sweet. It is not he that reads most but he that meditates most that will prove to be the

choicest, sweetest, wisest and strongest Christian.[12]

For some, the word "meditation" conjures up images of transcendental meditation or various forms of New Age meditative practices. What is the difference between these forms of meditation and biblical meditation? As Peter Toon says,

> The simplest way to highlight the difference is to say that for the one meditation is an inner journey to find the centre of one's being, while for the other it is the concentration of the mind/heart upon an external Revelation. For the one revelation/insight/illumination occurs when the inmost self (which is also the ultimate Self, the one final Reality) is reached by the journey into the soul, while for the other it comes as a result of encounter with God in and through his objective Revelation to which Holy Scripture witnesses.[13]

In other words, the Christian believer meditates on God and His truth, while a New Age practitioner attempts to go deeper into the self. While New Age meditation should be avoided, biblical meditation should be fully embraced as a spiritual practice.

---

[12] Tarrants, Thomas A. "Biblical Meditation." *C.S. Lewis Institute*, 2019, www.cslewisinstitute.org/Biblical_Meditation.

[13] Toon, Peter. *Meditating as a Christian* (London: HarperCollins, 1991), 18-19.

As Joshua is about to conquer the Promised God, God says to him, "Keep this Book of the Law always on your lips; meditate on it day and night, so that you may be careful to do everything written in it. Then you will be prosperous and successful" (Joshua 1:8, NIV). Meditation on God's truth is meant to be a consistent practice in the life of the believer, as we can see from the Psalms:

> Blessed is the one who does not walk in step with the wicked or stand in the way that sinners take or sit in the company of mockers, but whose delight is in the law of the Lord, and who meditates on his law day and night (Psalm 1:1-2, NIV).
>
> Within your temple, O God, we meditate on your unfailing love (Psalm 48:9, NIV).
>
> I will consider all your works and meditate on all your mighty deeds (Psalm 77:12, NIV).
>
> I reach out for your commands, which I love, that I may meditate on your decrees (Psalm 119:48, NIV).

We meditate on God's decrees because His thoughts are higher than our thoughts, and His ways are higher than our ways. When we meditate, we receive His decrees and become one with them internally. He writes them on the tablet of our heart.

Here are some practical steps in the process of biblical meditation[14]:

- **Silence**: Quiet your mind by taking time to silently focus your thoughts on a chosen passage of Scripture (or on the decree that you have received from the Lord).
- **Reading**: Slowly read a short passage of the selected Scripture aloud several times. Allow its words and their meanings to sink into your soul.
- **Meditation**: Meditation is like chewing. It involves slowly and completely tasting the thought or idea on which you are fixated. Ask yourself questions like, "What is God saying?" Place yourself in the passage of Scripture and ask God to examine you. Hum or sing the Scripture in faith that your entire being would be filled with the Word.
- **Prayer**: Pray using the passage as an outline for your prayer. Read the passage phrase-by-phrase, responding to God after each phrase or verse.
- **Contemplation**: Wait in silence and stillness once more. Listen for Holy Spirit, and allow Him to guide or illumination your mind/heart regarding areas of your life that He is transforming. Contemplate God's love, truth, and power as it is revealed to you.
- **Practice**: Find Scriptural ways of expressing the Word upon which you have meditated.

The goal of meditation is to <u>become</u> the message - to become the decree. It's not about ruminating over "dead letter." It's about becoming the Living Word.

---

[14] Tarrants, Thomas A. "Biblical Meditation." *C.S. Lewis Institute*, 2019, www.cslewisinstitute.org/Biblical_Meditation. (Some of this material was adapted from this source.)

Practical Example:

In Joe's case from earlier, you would spend time meditating on God's decree of peace for Joe, using these principles of biblical meditation to become one with that decree.

4. Declaration

Once we have confessed and meditated upon the divine decree, we are now ready to declare what God has decreed. A declaration is a formal or explicit announcement, accounting, or statement of fact that affirms the state or condition of a thing, an individual, or a community. In our context, a declaration is a prophetic announcement about what God has already decreed.

The Apostle Paul wrote, "Pray also for me, that whenever I speak, words may be given me so that I will fearlessly make known the mystery of the gospel, for which I am an ambassador in chains. Pray that I may declare it fearlessly, as I should" (Ephesians 6:19-20, NIV). We declare the words that are given to us by God, and we declare them fearlessly. For God has said, "I make known the end from the beginning, from ancient times, what is still to come. I say, 'My purpose will stand, and I will do all that I please'" (Isaiah 46:10, NIV). When we know what God has decreed, we can be very bold in our declarations. For example, because the prophet Elijah prayed and knew the decrees of God, he could say that it would not rain except by his word.

When we are making declarations, we are essentially painting a picture of what God's decree will look like when it fully manifests. Like God Himself, we are "world building" with our words. We are describing the effect of God's decree with as much skill, detail, and specificity as possible. This involves opening up our prophetic imagination to receive images and information from God, then relaying that message to the object of our declaration.

When it comes to declarations, the question for the believer becomes, "What does this decree look like in real time? How much can you articulate? How much detail can you provide? How vivid of a picture can you paint?" The power of the divine decree will flow in the area of your declaration. Like the branch that receives its life from the vine, your declarations will allow the divine life to flow through you and bear fruit. May it be unto you according to your faith!

Practical Example:

Once you have confessed and meditated on God's decree of peace for Joe, once you have become one with it in your spirit, you are ready to declare that new reality to Joe. Remember, this declaration is like painting a new reality in Joe's world.

As led by the inspiration of Holy Spirit, you might say something like this: "Joe, by the authority invested in me by the Lord Jesus Christ, I declare the PEACE of God over your life. From the time you were young, you didn't know how to heal from the trauma you experienced, and you grappled with a great deal of anxiety when you got older, but God says, 'No more!' He has come to heal you today.

You are going to experience a peace from God that surpasses comprehension. He is bringing a settled calm to all the storms that have been raging on the inside. Just as Jesus commanded the physical storm to still, He is saying, "Peace, be still" to all the chaos inside. The tension in your body is going to dissipate, and for the first time in a long time, you are going to sleep peacefully at night. Peace that you haven't experienced since you were a young child - it's yours in the mighty name of Jesus. This peace is going to rewire your brain and regulate your emotions. You are going to have the healthiest relationships you've ever had. All the love that's really in your heart is going to be expressed, and God is going to mend so many things that have been broken. As your spirit shifts, new doors of opportunity are going to open up to you, and the dream of God for your life will manifest. And you will be an ambassador of God's peace to so many in your generation who are full of stress and anxiety. When you walk into a room, your spirit will be so full of God's peace that it will bring a settled calm to everything around you. And because of this peace, everything under your care will flourish and bring forth new life. In Jesus' name!"

5. Proclamation

A proclamation is a public, official announcement and expression regarding the proceeding will of God for individuals and a community. It is an open statement regarding the decree(s) of God. For a historical example, think of the Emancipation Proclamation which publicly declared freedom to all slaves held in the southern states.

> **Practical Example:**
>
> In Joe's case, one might draw up an official document that can be displayed in his home - an open, public statement that reflects God's decree of peace for his life. This proclamation may also include a detailed declaration of that decree.

6. Renouncement

Successfully getting the will of God from heaven to earth will often involve renouncements. To "renounce" is to give up a claim, belief, or practice; to refuse further association with something; to refuse to follow; to break legal ties with a demonic covenant; or to formally resign.

Jesus said to His disciples, "If any one desires to follow me, let him renounce self and take up his cross, and so be my follower" (Matthew 16:24, WNT). Paul writes to Titus, "For the grace of God has appeared, bringing salvation to all people. It trains us to renounce ungodly living and worldly passions so that we might live sensible, honest, and godly lives in the present age" (Titus 2:11-12, ISV).

> **Practical Example:**
>
> If you are publicly ministering to Joe, you may make some renouncements on his behalf. In a more private setting, you would assist Joe in making those renouncements for himself. Either way, the

power comes when Joe agrees and "buys in" to what you are saying. Let's say you are ministering publicly:

"Lord Jesus, on behalf of Joe, I renounce all forms of anxiety. That stronghold is broken in the name of Jesus, and we break all legal ties with it. We renounce chaos and confusion. We renounce inordinate anger, frustration, and depression. Those things are cut off in Jesus' name. Every curse is broken. We refuse all association with these things, and they are powerless in Joe's world."

7. Promise

A promise is "a declaration, written or verbal, made by one person to another, which binds the person who makes it to do, or to forbear to do, a specified act."[15] In a biblical sense, a promise is an announcement legally guaranteed by God that He will do a particular thing or that a particular thing will happen. A promise from God is a legal oath derived from a need and focused on a result.

The Scriptures are replete with promises from God, as the Apostle Peter notes:

> Grace and peace be multiplied to you in the knowledge of God and of Jesus our Lord, as His divine power has given to us all things that pertain to life and godliness, through

---

[15] "promise." *Definitions.net.* STANDS4 LLC, 2022. Web. 2 Apr. 2022. <https://www.definitions.net/definition/promise>.

the knowledge of Him who called us by glory and virtue, by which have been given to us exceedingly great and precious promises, that through these you may be partakers of the divine nature, having escaped the corruption that is in the world through lust (2 Peter 1:2-4, NKJV).

These "exceedingly great and precious promises" are throughout the Scriptures, and the more we are aware of these promises, the more we can access them and activate them by faith. God has promised that He would never leave us or forsake us, that He would work all things together for the good of those who love God, that He would supply all our needs according to His riches in glory, and so much more! When you as a minister announce or declare the promises of God to a person, you are building their faith and strengthening their spirit so that they can receive the decrees of God that you are declaring over their life.

It must be noted, however, that some promises are unilateral (unconditional) and others are bilateral or multilateral (conditional). There are some things that God promises to do simply because He is God. There are other things that are dependent on our posture before Him or on our decisions. God does not break His promises, but if the promise being referenced is a conditional promise, then sometimes that promise can be suspended until the conditions of the promise are met.

For example, living on the "drama triangle" is one way to keep some of the promises of God from coming to pass in your life. The drama triangle consists of the persecutor, the victim, and the ally. When someone feels offended by someone else, they may assume the role of a victim, while making the other person out to be the persecutor. The victim may then seek out an ally to help launch an assault on the persecutor. The persecutor may then feel offended and assume the role of the victim, producing another triangle. Eventually, if left unchecked, the first triangle can spawn a never-ending fractal of more and more triangles. The way to escape the drama triangle is to assume the role of the "sovereign" - the one who refuses to participate in the drama. Instead, this person seeks the counsel of the Lord and releases the decrees of heaven in the situation.

Practical Example:

You are continuing to minister to Joe. Remember that the purpose of reminding Joe of God's promise is to build his faith and strengthen his spirit to the point where he can receive everything you are saying.

"Joe, God has promised that He would never leave you or forsake you. He never left you, and He never will. He is with you right now. He sees you right where you are, He knows you fully, and He loves you unconditionally. He is going to cause all things to work together for good in your life. You never have to be afraid, for the God of the universe - the one who loves you - is always with you."

8. Impartation

As noted in Chapter 6, impartation is the transference of gifts from one person to another through the laying on of hands or other means. It involves the ability to give others that which God has allocated for them, and it rapidly accelerates spiritual growth. By receiving impartation, believers can experience a "quantum leap" in their spiritual journey as they learn from the Spirit of God in those with decades of experience. Ideally, growth by impartation should be a reality experienced by every single believer.

Impartation is often related to "transfer of spirits." After Moses commissioned Joshua, his successor, to lead the children of Israel, it was said that "Joshua the son of Nun was full of the spirit of wisdom, for Moses had laid his hands on him" (Deuteronomy 34:9, ESV). Moses imparted a spirit of wisdom to Joshua so that he could lead the people effectively. Similarly, the prophet Elisha, the protege of Elijah, received a "double portion" of Elijah's spirit.

The Apostle Paul said, "I long to see you so that I may impart to you some spiritual gift to make you strong" (Romans 1:11, NIV). We, too, should long to impart what God has allocated for other believers - and to receive impartation, as well.

Practical Example:

If you are carrying God's peace in your spirit and God leads you to impart this peace to Joe, you might lay hands on him and invite him to receive this impartation of peace.

9. Regulation

A regulation is a statute, rule, or directive given by God to preserve life and maintain blessing. The book of Leviticus, for example, contains many regulations that the priests of that time needed to adhere to in order to properly facilitate God's presence in the tabernacle. After Nadab and Abihu were consumed by fire for offering unauthorized fire in the presence of the Lord, the Lord said to Aaron (the high priest),

> You and your sons are not to drink wine or other fermented drink whenever you go into the tent of meeting, or you will die. This is a lasting ordinance for the generations to come, so that you can distinguish between the holy and the common, between the unclean and the clean, and so you can teach the Israelites all the decrees the Lord has given them through Moses (Leviticus 10:9-11, NIV).

The Lord put a regulation in place in order to preserve the lives of the priests, to teach the nation the difference between the sacred and the common, and to maintain the blessing of God on the priesthood and the nation.

Divinely inspired regulations are relational in nature, and they act as "glory guards" - preserving that which is good, sacred, and beautiful in the relationship. Consider, for example, the covenant of marriage. There are certain regulations that each party willingly chooses to adhere to in order to maintain the sanctity, security, and blessing of the marital relationship. They agree to be faithful to one another, to love one another, and to be together for as long as they both shall live. The purpose of these regulations is not restriction; it is preservation.

When God wants to release blessing in someone's life at another level, there will often (if not always) be certain regulations that must be kept in order to maintain that level of blessing. However, it must be noted that these regulations come by revelation. To attempt to enforce regulations without revelation will inevitably result in legalism and bondage, but revelation combined with the associated divinely inspired regulations will result in the manifestation of God's glory. Once again, revelation + regulation = manifestation.

Practical Example:

God may give you certain regulations that Joe must follow in order to maximize the benefits of God's decree of peace for his life. The first may be that Joe must stop cursing his life; he must begin to speak the will of God over his life and agree with what God has said concerning him. The second might be that Joe must seek out a Spirit-filled professional counselor and begin therapy to unpack some of his childhood trauma.

10. Reconciliation

Reconciliation is the action of making an individual (or community) one or compatible with God by redemptive exchange. It involves bringing two or more parties back into a harmonious relationship. The Apostle Paul writes,

> Therefore, if anyone is in Christ, the new creation has come: The old has gone, the new is here! All this is from God, who reconciled us to himself through Christ and gave us the ministry of reconciliation: that God was reconciling the world to himself in Christ, not counting people's sins against them. And he has committed to us the message of reconciliation. We are therefore Christ's ambassadors, as though God were making his appeal through us. We implore you on Christ's behalf: Be reconciled to God. God made him who had no sin to be sin for us, so that in him we might become the righteousness of God (2 Corinthians 5:17-21, NIV).

Reconciliation is extremely important to God, and He is continually drawing us into reconciliation with Himself and with one another. Jesus even instructs worshippers to reconcile with their brothers or sisters before offering their gifts to God (see Matthew 5:21-26). The Apostle Peter instructs husbands to be considerate to their wives so that nothing would hinder their prayers (see 1 Peter 3:7).

Our relationships with one another are critical, and sometimes, in order for the decrees and promises of God to fully manifest, there is reconciliation work that must be done. We must pray and work diligently to restore broken relationships, to forgive those who have offended us, and to repent when we have injured others. When we get back into right relationship with God and others, the blessings of God will flow at another level!

Practical Example:

With God:
The daily practice of reconciliation with God involves actively exchanging with Christ - our weakness for His strength, our death for His life, our darkness for His light, our sorrow for His joy, etc. In prayers and daily devotions, Joe must "trade" with God - surrendering the various aspects of the old human nature and receiving all the spiritual blessings that are in Christ.

With others:
Part of the declaration that was released over Joe was that he would have healthy relationships and that God would mend things that were broken. As Joe receives God's decree of peace, he may be led to reconcile with family members, friends, or even enemies in his life. This will allow the peace of God to flow more fully in his world.

11. Petition

A prayer of petition involves appealing to God with respect to a particular cause. To petition is "to make a prayer or request to; to ask from; to solicit; to entreat; especially, to make a formal written supplication, or application to, as to any branch of the government; as, to petition the court; to petition the governor."[16] In our context, a petition is a formal request submitted to God that hits the target with regard to a particular issue or situation.

In Scripture, we are given this instruction: "Do not be anxious about anything, but in every situation, by prayer and petition, with thanksgiving, present your requests to God. And the peace of God, which transcends all understanding, will guard your hearts and your minds in Christ Jesus" (Philippians 4:6-7, NIV). We are invited and encouraged to consistently bring our petitions to God in every situation. The Apostle Paul writes in another place, "pray in the Spirit on all occasions with all kinds of prayers and requests" (Ephesians 6:18a, NIV).

To bring the will of God to the earth, to manifest His decrees, we must become skilled in the art of submitting formal petitions to God. The most effective petitions involve intercession that "hits the bullseye" - prayers that align with the heart and will of God. The Apostle John says, "This is the confidence we have in approaching God: that if we ask anything according to his will, he hears us. And if we know that he hears us—whatever we ask—we know that we have what we asked of him" (1 John 5:14-15, NIV).

Several individuals in Scripture (e.g., Daniel) had regimented times of prayer throughout the day. There were also collective hours of prayer and even "night watches." Though we are encouraged to pray without ceasing in the New Testament, it is helpful to dedicate certain times of prayer to God for the purpose of focused

---

[16] "petition." *Definitions.net*. STANDS4 LLC, 2022. Web. 2 Apr. 2022. <https://www.definitions.net/definition/petition>.

intercession. On many occasions, we have not because we ask not. Sometimes, the only thing holding up the next blessing or breakthrough from God is the right petition.

Practical Example:

For Joe, part of manifesting God's peace in his life may involve submitting regular petitions to God regarding challenges that arise. Instead of anxiously worrying, getting angry, or becoming depressed, Joe can begin seeking the will of God and articulating his requests. As Joe submits his petitions, combined with gratitude for God's goodness, his confidence in God will rise, and the peace of God will continue to guard his heart and mind in Christ Jesus.

12. Allocation

An allocation is a portion of resources assigned by God to a particular recipient for a divine purpose. When God issues a divine decree, there is always an allocation associated with that decree that assists the recipient in bringing the will of God to pass. This allocation may involve finances, connections, relationships, property, opportunities, etc.

In Scripture, a person's allocation is sometimes referred to as their portion, their cup, or their lot. When the nation of Israel conquered the Promised Land, the land was divided to each tribe according to their lot as an inheritance. David wrote, "Lord, you alone are my portion and my cup; you make my lot secure. The boundary lines have fallen for me in pleasant places; surely I have a delightful inheritance" (Psalm 16:5-6, NIV).

Our God is Jehovah Jireh - the Lord who sees and provides - and He has promised that He would supply all our needs according to His riches in glory. We have a heavenly bank account and an opportunity to store up treasures in heaven. When we use our resources well, we can open up heaven - just like Cornelius who, by prayers and gifts to the poor, prompted God to respond with an angelic visitation (see Acts 10).

When ministering to someone, God may provide you with insight as to His divine allocation for that person. Communicating this to the individual will often help to increase their faith and embolden them to receive what God has for them.

Practical Example:

Let's say you are still publicly ministering to Joe. Part of that ministry may involve describing certain allocations from God that belong to him: "Joe, when you receive this peace from the Lord, there are open doors of opportunity that are waiting for you. They have your name on them, and they belong to you. And God will supply every resource you need in order to accomplish His purpose. You are entering the most productive years of your life, and God has even assigned certain people to come alongside you to help implement the vision that God has given you. And in the next three years, God is going to open the way to home ownership, and it will be a sign that God is establishing you. Receive it in Jesus' name!"

13. Dedication

Dedication is the act of devoting something to God for His purpose alone. When something is dedicated to God, it is set apart and declared holy for God's particular use. We must practice dedicating ourselves, our families, and everything in our worlds to God.

God told Moses to tell the Israelites, "Make an altar of earth for me and sacrifice on it your burnt offerings and fellowship offerings, your sheep and goats and your cattle. Wherever I cause my name to be honored, I will come to you and bless you" (Exodus 20:24, NIV). Whenever we properly dedicate something to God, we associate His Name (His essence, character, and reputation) with that particular thing, and He commits to blessing it for His Name's sake. If we commit our works to the Lord, our plans will prosper under His hand, according to His will.

When King Solomon dedicated the temple to God, he "offered a sacrifice of twenty-two thousand head of cattle and a hundred and twenty thousand sheep and goats" (2 Chronicles 7:5, NIV). Part of God's response to this dedication was, "I have chosen and consecrated this temple so that my Name may be there forever. My eyes and my heart will always be there" (2 Chronicles 7:16, NIV), as long as Solomon and the people continued to walk faithfully before Him.

Practical Example:

After receiving this powerful word about God's peace for his life, let's say Joe goes back home to his studio apartment. He wants the peace of God to dwell not only in him but in everything in his sphere of influence, so he begins to dedicate (or re-dedicate) his life and his living space to God: "Father, in the name of Jesus, I dedicate my life to You. It belongs to You, Lord. Put Your Name on my life, and use it for Your purpose. My life is holy unto the Lord. It is set apart for You. I also dedicate this apartment to You. Let it likewise be used for Your purpose. May Your peace dwell in this atmosphere. Saturate everything with Your presence, in Jesus' name."

14. Vow

Closely associated with the act of dedication is the act of making a vow. A vow is a solemn promise to do something in response to something God has done or will do. Vow-making is a way to activate both the grace of God in human affairs and the dutiful response of the child of God to His goodness. Here is a prominent example from Scripture:

> Then Jacob made a vow, saying, "If God will be with me and will watch over me on this journey I am taking and will give me food to eat and clothes to wear so that I return safely to my father's household, then the Lord will be my God and this stone that I have set up as a pillar will be God's house,

and of all that you give me I will give you a tenth" (Genesis 28:20-22, NIV).

A vow made to God is a solemn and holy act, and it binds a person to their word. Numbers 30:2 (NIV) says, "When a man makes a vow to the Lord or takes an oath to obligate himself by a pledge, he must not break his word but must do everything he said." In the Scriptures, Hannah asked God to open her womb, and she vowed that if God gave her a son, she would dedicate him back to God in service. After God gave her a son, she was bound to fulfill the oath that she made, and she dedicated Samuel to God. A vow binds a person to pious, dutiful action in response to the actions of God.

A vow also unites a person to God with regard to a particular project or situation, binding their soul to Him. The word "vow" comes from the Latin word *votum*, from which we derive the English word "vote." A vow in the Kingdom of God is in many ways analogous to a vote in human governments. During a political campaign in a human government, a voter may say to a candidate, "I will give you my vote if you make something happen for me." In the Kingdom of God, our vows prompt or provoke God to activate resources on our behalf.

Paying our vows also gives legitimacy to what we decree and declare. "You will make your prayer to Him, He will hear you, And you will pay your vows. You will also declare a thing, And it will be established for you; So light will shine on your ways" (Job 22:27-28, NKJV).

Practical Example:

Inspired by the declaration that was given to him regarding the peace of God, Joe may choose to activate this reality by making a vow to the Lord: "God, if You do all that was spoken - if You bring peace to my life, my relationships, and my body - then I will be an ambassador of that peace wherever You send me."

15. Blessing

A blessing is the interposition of good into the life of another. To bless is to pronounce or invoke God's divine life and favor that works to enhance the life or situation of another. It is asking God by His Spirit to come and augment or transform people. When we bless someone, it is the expression of our will united with the will of God for the benefit of another. Similarly, a benediction is far from simply a prayer at the end of a service; properly defined, is the invocation or bestowing of a blessing.

In the Old Testament, God instructed Aaron and his sons to bless the people of Israel in this way: "The Lord bless you and keep you; the Lord make his face shine on you and be gracious to you; the Lord turn his face toward you and give you peace" (Numbers 6:24-26, NIV). What a powerful blessing! And because of Christ, "praise be to the God and Father of our Lord Jesus Christ, who has blessed us in the heavenly realms with every spiritual blessing in Christ" (Ephesians 1:3, NIV).

The Greek word "eulogeó" (from which we derive the word "eulogy") means to bless, speak well of, or praise. It involves speaking with a divinely convicted heart filled with the predetermined counsel of God. We must practice pronouncing blessings over our families, our neighbors, and all that is in our sphere of influence.

Practical Example:

When ministering to Joe, the Spirit of God may lead you to pronounce a blessing over his life: "Joe, may God bless you with peace that goes beyond your wildest dreams. May you experience the security, stability, and settledness that comes from knowing that God is with you. May this peace dwell in you so richly that everything prospers under your hand. May you be graced by God to heal that which is broken and to bring people together for cooperative purpose. May this grace open many doors for you, and may you be an ambassador of the peace of God. May God empower you to resolve conflicts that others said could not be resolved. May your eyes be opened to all the color, life, and beauty in the world around you, and may your heart rejoice in God's abundant goodness. May joy fill your heart and bubble up into laughter. May every wound be healed and every tear wiped from your eyes. May God pour out the oil of gladness over your head and over your life and over your relationships, in Jesus' name!"

16. Activation

Activation is the process of making something operative in the purposes of God. It may involve removing spiritual, emotional, or mental roadblocks, or it may involve providing the conditions necessary for the expression of certain spiritual gifts within a person. Paul told Timothy to "fan into flame the gift of God, which is in you through the laying on of my hands" (2 Timothy 1:6, NIV).

Practical Example:

Let's say it's been three years since the decree of God's peace was released over Joe's life, and let's say that Joe has been actively receiving and walking in that decree. There is tremendous fruit in his life, and now you sense that God wants to activate him within the church community in the area of conflict resolution. This may involve training and discipleship - perhaps allowing Joe to work alongside a leader who is already actively doing this work. Eventually, Joe will be released to fully operate in this area, expressing the grace that God has given him.

17. Confirmation

Confirmation is the verification or final proof of the Godly state of a person's life and position. It speaks to the fruit of a person's character, gift, or calling. The Apostle Peter said, "Therefore, my brothers and sisters, make every effort to confirm your calling and election. For if you do these things, you will never stumble, and you will receive a rich welcome into the eternal kingdom of our Lord and Savior Jesus Christ" (2 Peter 1:10-11, NIV).

A public confirmation may involve a ceremony or rite of passage that affirms God's gift or calling in a person's life or designates them to a particular office within the church or organization.

Practical Example:

It's been five years since the decree, and Joe has been actively working in the church's conflict resolution ministry. Cases are being resolved, and estranged parties are renewing their relationships. According to the guidance of Holy Spirit, perhaps the church leader will consecrate Joe as an elder within the church - publicly confirming the work that God is doing in and through Joe.

12 - Conducting Casework

Now that we have all these tools of the trade in our toolbox, how do we utilize them to co-rule with Christ? How do we apply them to our daily lives - to our personal challenges, our relationships, our finances, our families, our neighborhoods, and our communities? When things happen on the journey, how do we respond? How do we co-rule with Christ?

In real life situations, co-ruling with Christ often involves conducting "casework" - investigating and collecting data about a situation, doing a comprehensive analysis to arrive at an inspired judgment or diagnosis, and establishing a treatment plan utilizing the tools of the trade.

How to Conduct Casework

In some situations, ministry to an individual is isolated to a moment at a church service or a prayer at the altar. In these kinds of situations, God may provide you with insight regarding a divine decree for that person's life - in which case, you can then use the various tools of the trade, as led by Holy Spirit, to declare what God has decreed and minister to that individual.

However, in situations that are more "in-depth" or "long-term," you will need to conduct more extensive casework. There are three main components to conducting spiritual casework:

1. Investigation (Data Collection)

2. Comprehensive Analysis and Diagnosis
3. Treatment Plan

Investigation (Data Collection): The investigation stage involves gathering as much helpful information as possible about a situation. Ask all kinds of questions:

- Does this person acknowledge Jesus Christ as Savior and Lord?
- Is this person filled with Holy Spirit?
- What are the person's patterns and operating systems?
- What are their habits and behaviors?
- How is their spiritual, emotional, mental, and physical state of being?
- What is the person connected to (other people, places, things, ideas, belief systems, organizations, etc.)?
- Does the person require inner healing or deliverance?
- Is the person using any prescribed medication?
- Is the person using any harmful substances?
- What damage or trauma has the person sustained in their lifetime?
- What do they believe is possible regarding their situation?
- Does the person want to be made whole?

Comprehensive Analysis and Diagnosis: The analysis stage involves synthesizing all the data to arrive at a divinely inspired judgment or diagnosis about the situation. This process involves using discernment and recognizing patterns or prominent issues that rise to the surface. At some point, the minister brings the situation before the Lord and receives His divine decree from the Heavenly Council.

Treatment Plan: Once the decree from the Lord has been received, the minister must confess and meditate on the decree until they embody this judgment from the Lord. With the help of Holy Spirit, the minister then creates a "treatment plan" for the individual - a plan that utilizes the tools of the trade. This will often involve addressing the arguments in people's minds that may be in opposition to God's decree about their situation. Like an attorney prosecuting a case, the minister must overcome the person's internal arguments that would hinder them from receiving what God has for them. The minister must convince the person to "buy in" to God's reality.

How to Utilize the Tools of the Trade

In thinking about how to utilize the tools of the trade, it will be helpful to continue to consider the metaphor of physical tools in a toolbox. Not every household task requires the use of every tool. For one task, you might need a ruler, a saw, and a power drill. For another task, you might just need a hammer and a nail. Understanding the purposes of the various tools, as well as understanding what the task requires, will allow you to utilize the tools effectively.

In a similar way, not every spiritual tool of the trade needs to be utilized in every situation, and often, the order in which they are used depends on the situation, as well. There are some basic principles, such as declaring what God has decreed, but the process is ultimately led by the inspiration and guidance of Holy Spirit. As you continue to build your skills with the various tools by putting them into practice, and as you stay open to the guidance of Holy Spirit, you will eventually learn how to flow with Him. Holy Spirit will prompt you and show you how to utilize all of these tools organically and naturally, according to how He has designed and anointed you.

The Man by the Pool of Bethesda

For an example of Jesus conducting casework, consider the story of the man by the pool of Bethesda:

> After this there was a feast of the Jews; and Jesus went up to Jerusalem. Now there is at Jerusalem by the sheep market a pool, which is called in the Hebrew tongue Bethesda, having five porches. In these lay a great multitude of impotent folk, of blind, halt, withered, waiting for the moving of the water. For an angel went down at a certain season into the pool, and troubled the water: whosoever then first after the troubling of the water stepped in was made whole of whatsoever disease he had. And a certain man was there, which had an infirmity thirty and eight years. When Jesus saw him lie, and knew that he had been now a long time in that case, he saith unto him, Wilt thou be made whole? The impotent man answered him, Sir, I have no man, when the water is troubled, to put me into the pool: but while I am coming, another

steppeth down before me. Jesus saith unto him, Rise, take up thy bed, and walk. And immediately the man was made whole, and took up his bed, and walked: and on the same day was the sabbath (John 5:1-9, KJV).

<u>Investigation (Data Collection)</u>: Jesus saw this man lying by the pool of Bethesda, and He knew that the man had been in that case for a long time. He then asked the man if he was willing to be made whole - if he earnestly desired to be healed. Jesus was investigating the man's situation, as well as his faith and internal posture.

<u>Comprehensive Analysis and Diagnosis</u>: The man's response revealed his mentality. He had an established argument in his mind for why he could not be made whole. After 38 years of infirmity, he said he could not be made whole because he had no one to put him in the water.

<u>Treatment Plan</u>: Jesus addressed this man's case by commanding him to rise, take up his bed, and walk. He overcame the argument in the man's mind, invited him to place his faith in the Healer, and ultimately, caused the man to experience miraculous wholeness.

Closing Remarks

It is my hope and prayer that every believer would awaken to the unlimited possibilities associated with our current position and seat with Christ in heavenly places. In the same way that a sitting president or judge is granted power to govern and make a difference in the lives of those they serve, we too have been empowered to give witness to the resurrection and Lordship of Christ Jesus by overturning inferior demonic and human judgments.

Unfortunately, there are several detrimental, nefarious things that have been normalized by a part of our current church culture. It also appears that some have even grown comfortable with things our Lord considered intolerable. Nevertheless, the foundation of God stands sure. God has always had a witness in every generation, and I am persuaded that He will have no less in this current one. The Lord showed me thousands of believers using their faith, not to coddle satanic tyranny or seek to make a name for themselves, but to provide irrefutable and infallible proof of His resurrection and Lordship by restoring His just rule to people. We are called not only to preach the resurrection and Lordship of Jesus Christ, but more importantly, to demonstrate His life.

I believe many of you reading this book are a part of our Lord's remnant Church who shall follow His example by doing Kingdom casework. Consider our Lord's approach and mentality regarding the woman who was suffering from a grievous affliction for eighteen years:

> On a Sabbath Jesus was teaching in one of the synagogues, and a woman was there who had been crippled by a spirit for eighteen years. She was bent over and could not straighten up at all. When Jesus saw her, he called her forward and said to her, "Woman, you are set free from your infirmity." Then he put his hands on her, and immediately she straightened up and praised God. Indignant because Jesus had healed on the Sabbath, the synagogue leader said to the people, "There are six days for work. So come and be healed on those days, not on the Sabbath." The Lord answered him, "You hypocrites! Doesn't each of you on the Sabbath untie your ox or donkey from the stall and lead it out to give it water? Then should not this woman, a daughter of Abraham, whom Satan has kept bound for eighteen long years, be set free on the Sabbath day from what bound her?" When he said this, all his opponents were humiliated, but the people were delighted with all the wonderful things he was doing (Luke 13:10-17, NIV).

In verse 16 (KJV), Jesus says, "So ought not this woman, being a daughter of Abraham, whom Satan has bound—think of it—for eighteen years, be loosed from this bond on the Sabbath?" The term "ought" means "of necessity because of the case or situation." Jesus found it obligatory to heal her on the Sabbath (or any other day) due to the many factors that made up her case. Let's examine a few of those factors. First, Jesus said the woman was a daughter of Abraham, inferring her covenant right to the "children's bread." Second, He identified Satan as her captor for 18 years. Finally, He charged the religious institution of the day with being complicit in her bondage by exalting the traditions of men above the Word of God. In the final analysis, Jesus merely enforced in the earth, by His ruling, the things God had previously ruled from His Council in heaven.

I hope and pray that you receive the Lord's burden and His vision to restore His just rule to the earth by means of His death, burial, resurrection, ascension, and reign. I pray our Lord gives you someone who will mentor you - someone who will assist you with cultivating a good relationship with Holy Spirit and effectively using the tools of the trade. May our Lord equip you with everything you need to overthrow inferior demonic and human judgments by establishing His just rule in the earth.

Our Father who art in heaven, hallowed be thy name. Thy kingdom come. Thy will be done, on earth as it is in heaven. Give us this day our daily bread. And forgive us our debts, as we forgive our debtors. Lead us not into temptation, but deliver us from evil. For thine is the kingdom, and the power, and the glory, for ever and ever. Amen.

Acknowledgments

I would like to take this opportunity to express my sincere appreciation and gratitude to those who contributed to this project:

- Nathan Cole
- Melissa Walker

Appendix
The Five Laws of the Cross

The Five Laws of the Cross (Original Legislation)

As we mentioned in Chapter 7, we have crafted five pieces of "Kingdom legislation" to reflect the Five Laws of the Cross:

1. The Substitutionary Death and Emancipation Act
2. The Substitutionary Burial and Purification Act
3. The Substitutionary Resurrection and New Life Act
4. The Substitutionary Ascension and Spiritual Gifts Act
5. The Substitutionary Reign and Power Act

Each of these five acts articulates an aspect of what Christ accomplished on our behalf (and what we have access to as a result). Some modifications and additions were made to these pieces of legislation for the sake of the book format in Chapter 7, but we wanted to include them here in their original formats.

The Substitutionary Death and Emancipation Act

PREAMBLE

We the Senior Leadership of Embassy Covenant Church International, having received knowledge from the Word of God and the Heavenly Council, do hereby enact The Substitutionary Death and Emancipation Act. With this Kingdom legislation, we affirm the substitutionary death of our Lord Jesus Christ as divine judgment against sin, the carnal nature, the demonic kingdom, and the spirit of the world. We further affirm the resulting emancipation of humanity from all powers antithetical to the Kingdom of God, and we invite all people everywhere to personally identify with and experience the liberating power of the death of Jesus Christ - a power that will free individuals, families, communities, and nations.

THE CONDITION OF FALLEN HUMANITY

Human beings were created in the image of God and given a unique charge to govern the earth in God's stead, but Adam's rebellion tragically plunged all humanity into bondage. Fallen humanity was made subject to sin, the carnal nature, the demonic kingdom, and the spirit of the world - resulting in pain, suffering, violence, injustice, sickness, and death. In that fallen state, we were hopelessly unable to remedy our own condition.

THE SUBSTITUTIONARY DEATH OF JESUS CHRIST

God the Father demonstrated His infinite love, power, and wisdom by sending His only Son, Jesus Christ, to die on the cross as a representative of all humanity. The innocent was offered on behalf of the guilty, and this substitutionary sacrifice satisfied the righteous demands of God's justice and forever judged sin, the carnal nature, the demonic kingdom, and the spirit of the world - legally liberating humanity from these powers.

EXPERIENCING THE DEATH OF CHRIST

We manifest the tangible benefits of the death of Christ by believing, receiving, experiencing, and expressing this truth in the earth. As the Apostle Paul wrote, "I have been crucified with Christ and I no longer live, but Christ lives in me. The life I now live in the body, I live by faith in the Son of God, who loved me and gave himself for me" (Galatians 2:20, NIV). We must choose to carry our cross daily, reckon ourselves dead to sin, and allow the death of Christ to work within us, nullifying that which destroys. We activate the death of Christ by receiving it as a divine decree, confessing it, meditating on it, declaring it, and proclaiming/applying it to ourselves and to the world.

COMMUNITY IMPACT

Individuals, families, communities, and nations will benefit from The Substitutionary Death and Emancipation Act by identifying with Christ and partaking of this grace. "For if we have been united with him in a death like his, we shall certainly be united with him in a resurrection like his" (Romans 6:5, ESV). By activating this power, humanity will experience unprecedented freedom.

The Substitutionary Burial and Purification Act

PREAMBLE

We the Senior Leadership of Embassy Covenant Church International, having received knowledge from the Word of God and the Heavenly Council, do hereby enact The Substitutionary Burial and Purification Act. With this Kingdom legislation, we affirm the substitutionary burial of our Lord Jesus Christ as the effectual "putting away" of all human sin. We further affirm the resulting deliverance and complete purification of humanity, and we invite all believers everywhere to personally identify with and experience the purifying power of the burial of Jesus Christ - a power that brings complete freedom from all forms of bondage and cleanses us from all unrighteousness.

THE SUBSTITUTIONARY BURIAL OF JESUS CHRIST

After His death on the cross, Jesus Christ was buried on behalf of all humanity, and through this representative burial, He separated us from all sin, bondage, and corruption. In the burial of Christ, the record of sin was completely expunged and removed from us - as far as the east is from the west. It was buried in the burial of Christ. This burial also removed all negative influences, effects, and structures within us that resulted from our prior condition. They were dismantled, destroyed, and tossed into a sea of forgetfulness. Through the burial of Christ, God has purged us, washed us, and cleansed us from all unrighteousness, and He has legally liberated us from all demonic presence and power. Because of this burial, we are completely separated from the carnal nature, completely delivered from the bondage of the enemy, and completely purified from all corruption. We have a clear conscience, and no charges can be brought against us.

EXPERIENCING THE BURIAL OF CHRIST

We manifest the tangible benefits of the burial of Christ by believing, receiving, experiencing, and expressing this truth in the earth. The Apostle John wrote, "Dear friends, now we are children of God, and what we will be has not yet been made known. But we know that when Christ appears, we shall be like him, for we shall see him as he is. All who have this hope in him purify themselves, just as he is pure" (1 John 3:2-3, NIV). As believers, we are invited to participate in sanctification - the purification associated with the burial of Christ. We activate the power of this burial by receiving it as a divine decree, confessing it, meditating on it, declaring it, and proclaiming/applying it to ourselves and to the world.

COMMUNITY IMPACT

Individuals, families, communities, and nations will benefit from The Substitutionary Burial and Purification Act by identifying with Christ and partaking of this grace. "Blessed are the pure in heart, for they will see God" (Matthew 5:8, NIV). By activating this power, humanity will be redeemed from every lawless deed and purified as God's "own special people, zealous for good works" (Titus 2:14, NKJV).

The Substitutionary Resurrection and New Life Act

PREAMBLE

We the Senior Leadership of Embassy Covenant Church International, having received knowledge from the Word of God and the Heavenly Council, do hereby enact The Substitutionary Resurrection and New Life Act. With this Kingdom legislation, we affirm the substitutionary resurrection of our Lord Jesus Christ as the conclusive and incontestable triumph of God over death, hell, and the grave. We further affirm the resulting divine life available to humanity, and we invite all believers everywhere to personally identify with and experience this new life associated with the resurrection of Jesus Christ - a life that makes us partakers of the divine nature.

THE SUBSTITUTIONARY RESURRECTION OF JESUS CHRIST

Jesus Christ rose from the dead on behalf of all humanity, and through this representative resurrection, He forever conquered death, hell, and the grave. "And having disarmed the powers and authorities, he made a public spectacle of them, triumphing over them by the cross" (Colossians 2:15, NIV). Because of the resurrection of Christ, we too have triumphed over these powers, and we are subject to them no longer. "For the wages of sin is death; but the gift of God is eternal life through Jesus Christ our Lord" (Romans 6:23, KJV). Since we were united with Christ in His death, we were also united with Him in His resurrection. We are born from above, and we have been made partakers of the divine nature. Because of His resurrection, we live under an open heaven, and we have access to the nature, character, and Spirit of God.

EXPERIENCING THE RESURRECTION OF CHRIST

We manifest the tangible benefits of the resurrection of Christ by believing, receiving, experiencing, and expressing this truth in the earth. "We were buried therefore with him by baptism into death, in order that, just as Christ was raised from the dead by the glory of the Father, we too might walk in newness of life" (Romans 6:4, ESV). As believers, we are invited to participate in the new life of Christ - to "put on Christ" and allow Him to live through us. Through the resurrection of Christ, we have access to the manifold grace of God and the inexhaustible riches of Christ. This new life (and inheritance) begins now and continues throughout eternity. We activate the power of this resurrection by receiving it as a divine decree, confessing it, meditating on it, declaring it, and proclaiming/applying it to ourselves and to the world.

COMMUNITY IMPACT

Individuals, families, communities, and nations will benefit from The Substitutionary Resurrection and New Life Act by identifying with Christ and partaking of this grace. "Praise be to the God and Father of our Lord Jesus Christ! In his great mercy he has given us new birth into a living hope through the resurrection of Jesus Christ from the dead, and into an inheritance that can never perish, spoil or fade" (1

Peter 1:3-4a, NIV). By activating this power, humanity will triumph over death, hell, and the grave, and we will manifest the life of Christ in the earth.

The Substitutionary Ascension and Spiritual Gifts Act

PREAMBLE

We the Senior Leadership of Embassy Covenant Church International, having received knowledge from the Word of God and the Heavenly Council, do hereby enact The Substitutionary Ascension and Spiritual Gifts Act. With this Kingdom legislation, we affirm the substitutionary ascension of our Lord Jesus Christ as the unconditional acceptance of humanity in Christ. We further affirm the resulting spiritual gifts and mantles given to humanity, and we invite all believers everywhere to personally identify with and experience this ascension, with all its associated affirmation, glorification, and grace.

THE SUBSTITUTIONARY ASCENSION OF JESUS CHRIST

After His death, burial, and resurrection, Jesus ascended into heaven on our behalf and was seated at the right hand of the Father, far above all principality and power and every name that is named. He was completely accepted and embraced, and all things were put under his feet. As a glorified man with a glorified human nature, Christ Jesus represents all humanity before God, and in Him, we are accepted in the beloved and seated at the right hand of God. We are citizens of the Kingdom of God, and our spiritual residence is in heaven. From this position of authority, Christ also gave gifts to humanity, including the fivefold ministry gifts, the gifts of the Spirit, callings, anointings, assignments, and mantles - for the profit of the Church and the human race.

EXPERIENCING THE ASCENSION OF CHRIST

We manifest the tangible benefits of the ascension of Christ by believing, receiving, experiencing, and expressing this truth in the earth. "Since, then, you have been raised with Christ, set your hearts on things above, where Christ is, seated at the right hand of God. Set your minds on things above, not on earthly things. For you died, and your life is now hidden with Christ in God" (Colossians 3:1-3, NIV). Because of Christ's ascension, we can fully embrace our acceptance in God; and by faith, we can receive every spiritual gift that He has allocated for us, knowing that "we have different gifts, according to the grace given to each of us" (Romans 12:6a, NIV). We activate the power of this ascension by receiving it as a divine decree, confessing it, meditating on it, declaring it, and proclaiming/applying it to ourselves and to the world.

COMMUNITY IMPACT

Individuals, families, communities, and nations will benefit from The Substitutionary Ascension and Spiritual Gifts Act by identifying with Christ and partaking of this grace. Gifts from heaven, such as the fivefold ministry gifts (apostle, prophet, evangelist, pastor, teacher), will bless the earth tremendously on behalf of Christ. By activating the power of Christ's ascension, humanity will walk in tremendous acceptance and spiritual empowerment.

The Substitutionary Reign and Power Act

PREAMBLE

We the Senior Leadership of Embassy Covenant Church International, having received knowledge from the Word of God and the Heavenly Council, do hereby enact The Substitutionary Reign and Power Act. With this Kingdom legislation, we affirm the substitutionary reign of our Lord Jesus Christ that makes us co-rulers with Christ. We further affirm the resulting power and authority given to humanity in Christ, and we invite all believers everywhere to personally identify with and experience this reign so that we can be fully equipped and empowered to establish the Kingdom of God in the earth.

THE SUBSTITUTIONARY REIGN OF JESUS CHRIST

When Jesus ascended, the Father "seated him at his right hand in the heavenly realms, far above all rule and authority, power and dominion, and every name that is invoked, not only in the present age but also in the one to come. And God placed all things under his feet and appointed him to be head over everything for the church, which is his body, the fullness of him who fills everything in every way" (Ephesians 1:20b-23, NIV). And because we were in Christ when He ascended, "God raised us up with Christ and seated us with him in the heavenly realms in Christ Jesus" (Ephesians 2:6, NIV). In Him, we are ruling and reigning, and we have been given authority over all the power of the enemy. We are co-heirs with Christ who will inherit all things, and we are exercising governance and dominion for the glory of God - each of us according to our own measure of rule. This co-rulership begins in this life and continues throughout the ages.

EXPERIENCING THE REIGN OF CHRIST

We manifest the tangible benefits of the reign of Christ by believing, receiving, experiencing, and expressing this truth in the earth. Christ is ruling and reigning from the heavens, and by faith, we are reigning with Him, for in Him we live and move and have our being. We have the opportunity to seek God's counsel and hear His decrees so that we can manifest them in our world. Through co-rulership with Christ, we are partnering to bring God's Kingdom agenda to pass. We activate the power of this reign by receiving it as a divine decree, confessing it, meditating on it, declaring it, and proclaiming/applying it to ourselves and to the world.

COMMUNITY IMPACT

Individuals, families, communities, and nations will benefit from The Substitutionary Reign and Power Act by identifying with Christ and partaking of this grace. Through the reign of God's people in Christ, the Kingdom of God will come, and the will of God will be done on earth as it is in heaven. Christ will reign until all creation is made subject to Him and until all the kingdoms of the world have become the Kingdom of God; and His people will reign with Him forever and ever. By activating the power of Christ's reign, humanity will experience the limitless benefits associated with being under the rule of Christ.

Made in the USA
Coppell, TX
24 April 2023

16014535R00075